PRAIRIE WHISTLES

TALES OF MIDWEST RAILROADING

DENNIS BOYER

Trails Books
Black Earth, Wisconsin

10385045

Library of Congress Catalog Card Number: 2001087142
ISBN: 0-915024-90-X

Editor: Stan Stoga
Book Design: Heather Larson
Illustrations: Owen Coyle
Cover Design: John Huston
Cover Photos: Larry Michael (steam engine and depot)

Printed in the United States of America.

07 06 05 04 03 02 01   6 5 4 3 2 1

Trails Books, a division of Trails Media Group, Inc.
P.O. Box 317 • Black Earth, WI 53515
(800) 236-8088 • e-mail: info@wistrails.com
www.trailsbooks.com

In Memory of
Cream City Lodge #75, Brotherhood of Railway Carmen

CONTENTS

FOREWORD...vii

ACKNOWLEDGMENTS viii

PART ONE: BLOW THE WHISTLE AND RING THE BELL............1
Deadheading on the 381 2
All-American Engines 4
Railroad Boot Camp 7
Pullman Hanky-Panky..10
Timber Road 13
Steady As She Goes 15
Rolling the Distant Signal 19
Undercover Engine Trainee 21
"Easterners" 24
Wreck of the *Milwaukee*...27

PART TWO: GREASE, CINDERS, AND SIGNALS 31
Steamed Up 32
Epitaph for a Section Hand 34
High Altitude Railroading 36
Caboose No. 992094 39
Ties That Bind...42
Tender Boy 45
Tower Times 48
Oktoberfest Special 54
Accidental Carman 57
Working Section 60
Hospital Train 63
The Money Hole 66
Key Man 70
Shop Chicks 72

PART THREE: FELLOW TRAVELERS 77

Drover's Caboose 78

Tater Fraters 83

King Ole: Hobo Boss of the Midwest 86

Steaming Ore 89

Orphan Trains 92

Ghost Train 95

Little Boy's Eyes..............................97

Immigrant Train...............................99

Railroad Digs 101

Valley Characters 104

Railroad Canteen 107

Ship Jumper, Train Hopper 110

Fifty Years on the Bench 113

Honeymoon Train 115

Runaway Train 118

River City Layout 121

Lincoln's Depot 123

SOME RAILROADING TERMS 127

FOREWORD

Railroads occupy a special niche in the Midwest. Trains were the device by which our area was made a true crossroads of America. The interstate highways and the great air terminal hubs took their cues from the development and settlement patterns established by railroads.

Preserving railroad stories is a tricky matter. Rail history buffs have done quite a bit to memorialize the physical artifacts and the technical specifications from railroads of times past. Very little has been done to preserve the oral history of railroading subcultures.

Questions abound. How was railroading different from other blue-collar occupations in the industrial age? How did the various ethnic and immigrant groups interact with the railroads? What was the impact of rail arrival (and abandonment) on communities? Which parts of mind, heart, and soul were touched by train travel?

This collection does not definitively answer those questions. But it does represent my effort to broaden the railroad heritage dialogue beyond equipment and buildings. If it provokes compilations of stories about women railroaders, dining car menus, livestock transport, African-American track crews, railroad snow removal, labor strife, railroad car ferries, and the hundreds of activities and aspects in and about railroads, well, I would be a very happy rail fan.

A word of explanation is also in order. While I fancy myself something of a folklorist and have penned many a tall tale and collected a number of regional legends, this collection is a bit of a departure from the modus operandi used in my other books. Although these stories are infused with the humor and warmth of folktales, there is a strong case to be made that this collection stands apart in terms of the realism brought to the task by my narrators. It is, perhaps, more of a collection of reminiscences drawn from varying personal encounters with railroading. The reader will find heroes in these pages, but will also encounter the grit and wisdom that flows from my sources' experiences.

The collection is organized into three parts reflecting three interconnected themes: the operation of trains, the maintenance of the railroad systems, and the multifaceted interactions between humans and trains. Readers will soon see that these divisions are not artificial distinctions. Railroading, like many pursuits, has its caste systems, and the varied perspectives of this world naturally flow from the disparate vantage points of my observers.

And like many pursuits, railroading has its own colorful argot. To help readers with some of the terms in the collection, I've provided brief explanations of them at the end of the book.

Here's hoping that others will contribute what they know about ways that Midwest trains touched lives.

ACKNOWLEDGMENTS

A collection of oral reminiscences is, of course, dependent on the generosity of sources willing to share their insights and perspectives. The telling of tales to a stranger collecting stories is a form of intimacy that does not come easily to many people. The gifts of these tales to me, and thus to the reader, are doubly appreciated.

Most of my sources prefer, for a variety of reasons, to remain anonymous. I honor that request with some regret, hoping that friends and families will recognize these storytellers.

Beyond the direct sources, a collection such as this requires the guidance of those familiar with the cadence and content of railroad lore and the historical and sociological context of railroading communities. Dozens, if not hundreds, of encounters in the last twenty years helped shape my view of this subject matter. Naturally, the collection bears my interpretive stamp, and I alone bear responsibility for any liberties taken with the stories of others.

Special thanks to those who provided technical assistance and feedback: Eldon Behr, Owen Coyle, Tom Dwyer, Tony Hauser, Lincoln Johnson, Jeff Kehoe, Jack Kuhn, R. A. Landgraf, Dan Lanz, Carol Lewandowski, Dave Martens, Jeff Minton, Rick Murphy, Bill Nordgren, Harvey Paulson, Paul Reilly, Dick Richardson, Jerry Rosenow, Nathan Roth, Pete Schmidt, Bob Storozuk, John Strauss, Al Strayer, Steve Thompson, Corey Two Crow, Lysianne Unruh, Wanda Washington, Robert White, and Albert Zimmer. This appreciation is also extended generally to three fine railroad groups: the Milwaukee Road Historical Association, the Chicago & North Western Historical Society, and the Great Northern Railway Historical Society.

Thanks to Stan Stoga at Trails Media for encouraging this effort.

Finally, and most importantly, thanks to Donna Weikert, my long-suffering spouse, who will no longer have to endure stacks of rail photos, passenger schedules, depot blueprints, and rail yard maps covering every desk, table, and counter in our house.

PART ONE
Blow the Whistle and Ring the Bell.

Train crews are the most visible and romanticized elements of railroading. They once numbered among their ranks firemen, stewards, brakemen, cooks, switchmen, and busboys, in addition to today's conductors and engineers. It is a stratified and status conscious world, filled with pressures and responsibilities. It is also a world of satisfaction and pride at occupying the operative role in America's most honored industry.

DEADHEADING ON THE 381

Perhaps no category of railroad stories is more wistful and nostalgic than tales about a longtime worker's last day on the job. Retirement may spell welcome relief for many, garnished with opportunities to fish with grandchildren and more closely tend to the family farm. Yet even the weary among railroaders find the end to be bittersweet.

This story was perhaps one of the first railroad tales that I heard in the Midwest. It was definitely the first one that prompted note taking on my part. It arose in the atypical setting of a late 1970s wedding reception in Chicago with Nicholas, a long-retired Chicago & North Western engine fireman, telling a brand new Milwaukee Road carman what it was like in the steam era.

Much of what Nicholas said that day did not make sense at the time. Many of the nuances of his account were likely beyond my grasp and now beyond my memory. A host of details of a fireman's job life slipped through my fingers. I had no idea that this was a fabled train ride on one of America's premier routes. But it was impossible to miss the poignancy of the narrative concerning his last day.

Here it is, in the best form that I can recall and reconstruct. Nicholas, thanks for the memories!

Where did the years go? Seems like you're a young man one day and an old man the next. If you think back, you remember old people telling you how quick the years go. But you never believed them. Not at a time in your life when a week could drag out unbearably as long as dessert between you and your sweetheart. It's almost a scientific formula. When you're young, you're in a hurry, and when you're in a hurry time goes slowly.

It didn't really dawn on me until I put my hand on that grab iron and pulled myself up to the cab. I was done. Over thirty years of railroading was just about finished. Just one more ride, not even on the crew. Just a courtesy to an old-timer to let him deadhead down to St. Louis where I had family at that time.

I got on up here at Proviso Yards, just outside Chicago. It was a light version of the train 381, pulling about ninety-five cars. The 381 often towed over a hundred and twenty, with helper engines kicking in to push us through the rough country. It was three units to start with that day, F-7s. String of cars down out of Wisconsin and Upper Michigan, little bit of everything.

Orders came on the fly at the tower at Wolf Road. But you don't really make time until you get out of Proviso. You tangle with all sorts of switches, interconnections, and traffic around there. The fireman that day kept up a steady song of "red board" and "green board," his shouted announcements of yard signals. Red board was the signal to stop, and green board was the all-clear sign.

The F-7s that day were really vibrating. Those were shaky and loud units, especially in the engine compartment. It made me homesick for the old steamtrain, not the tremors of the F-7s. When I was still a real fireman, a shovel devil, I knew most of the locomotives just by the sound of the stroke. Each had its own voice in a combination of hums, steam sounds, and wheel clicks. You could pick them out like you could your kids singing in the dark.

This trip was the heart of the system. Gateway to the southern Illinois district by way of Dixon. Old railroad roots down that way. It was the frontier of railroading in the pioneer days, before the Mississippi bridges. Lots and lots of prime traffic from all sorts of connections. Everything from packed meat and I-beams to grain for breweries and toilet paper. In the old days you had local passenger service. But the dandies in my day were the through trains. The prime trains were the City of Portland and the Los Angeles Limited, shared traffic with the Union Pacific in those days.

We made a pickup at Meredith and they did a walking inspection. I went along with the front brakeman. Somebody said something about slop in the drawbars. They had the hills from Geneva to Nachusa to think about. So you want to run tight.

Sometimes that route went by way of the Lee County cutoff. That took you off the main line at Nachusa and back on at Nelson. It was used mainly to get out of the way of passenger trains or if the line was blocked. Then at Nelson you have the junction with the southern Illinois district of CNW. Crews change at the yard in Nelson and turn around to Proviso, sometimes on the 380. The 380 was the northbound twin of southbound 381 that day. Met it right at Nelson.

We dropped a few cars in Nelson. Something bound for Clinton, Iowa. Then it was off with a new crew, catching the running inspection out of the Nelson yard, and switching into the southern Illinois line. That was a tricky line that had its share of problems. Not as bad as some of those Mississippi Valley lines, but it had regular flood damage in my day. Bridge problems, levy washouts, and low track. Then you had the interaction with CRI&P and CB&Q. The Rock Island and the Burlington had their own problems and sometimes ran our line for emergencies.

No big problems on that last trip. Just lots of delays. It was like that coupler story jinxed the whole trip and was passed from crew to crew. Just a feeling that something wasn't quite right. I even wondered if it was me. Some crews thought it was bad luck to be with a fireman on his last trip. But it could have hardly been my fault that other traffic was bunched up under delay.

The Nelson crew kidded me a little. Engineer asked me if I was going to find a shovel somewhere, maybe stoke a furnace in a government building to make a little beer money. Brakeman asked me if I was going to miss the railroad. The eyes of the other crewmen fell on him like he had just cut a stinker in church. I didn't mind answering and I tried to be as honest as I could. I told him I'd miss some of it. I also told him it was a different breed of railroading that I was leaving from when I started. I missed steam most of all, especially on the last day. On that last day it was driven home that firemen are going the way of the passenger pigeon and the dodo bird. I told him that it's the feeling of a dying breed. It was real quiet in the cab after that.

In South Pekin there was another crew change and another running inspection. Funny, I had to answer all the same questions again. This time I kept it a little more lighthearted. I told them that at my age I was about as useful as an old coal tender and I wasn't about to have some greasy car-man steal parts off me or cut me up for scrap.

The South Pekin crew was an older bunch and we swapped stories down through Green Valley, Allen, Sweetwater, Barr, Virden, Girard and into the Benld yard. That's where trains switched control to the Litchfield and Madison system. From there it was a matter of crossing the Illinois Terminal railroad, running over the old Nickel Plate, and sharing track with the Illinois Central. At Madison, Illinois, you could see the haze of St. Louis.

I said my last good-byes to the CNW fellows at Madison. Picked up a transfer to the East St. Louis yard. From there I picked up a local passenger train into St. Louis. So I guess I was home. It didn't feel like home. Home was what I felt I left back at Proviso.

That was the end of deadheading for this old fireman. Haven't been up in a cab since. Haven't been near a freight since. My only train riding comes on the Amtrak. That's fine in its place. But whenever I do ride the passenger train it just takes me back to that last day, the day of deadheading down the southern Illinois division.

ALL-AMERICAN ENGINES

Locomotive power has fascinated rail fans since 1804, when British mining engineer Richard Trevithick made the first passenger run using a steam engine. Ever since, there has been an element of spectacle to the deployment and use of train engines. Captured in film, postcards, and song, the mechanical wonders of the rail age epitomized human optimism. No wonder politicians soon seized upon them as symbols of potency and efficiency, festooned them with flag bunting, and thereby blurred the lines between nationalism and industrialism.

While other nations have notable traditions concerning their locomotives, American railways have demanded much from their engines. The pressure has always been there for railroad locomotive power to live up to the brawny standards of American heavy industry. The engineering specifications have always heeded the North American sweep of topography and climate.

American engines have many fans, but none so steadfast as those who actually have held the throttle as a life's work. Among engineers there are those who approach the job with a hard-nosed work ethic and sniff at the notion of the romance of rail. But there also are those who view the railroad engine as a cowboy or cavalryman might view a horse, as partner and sentient being.

Wesley, a recently retired Chicago & North Western engineer, is among the hard core of engine devotees. A font of technical and anecdotal information, he holds court in a basement recreation room in Naperville. The walls are covered with photographs of engines. The bookshelves are lined with paperbacks, hardcovers, and ring binders connected to this cult of locomotive power. The air is thick with the talk of engines.

Engines forged this country! We'd still be a backwater if engines had not connected our various regions in time for us to be a world power as the old empires collapsed. Without the American railroad engine the rest of the world would be speaking German or Russian.

Right from the beginning of American rail, we're talking raw power and endurance. We're talking a whole continent here, a vast middle with long hauls, rough terrain, and some places inhospitable for man and machine. It's different than hauling ladies with parasols from Paris to Brussels, and it's different than carting yarn and parcels from Surrey to London.

I came into it right around the end of steam. Not that steam didn't have a place. But it could go only so far. The real contest, the real objective, is the quest for individual units with greater pulling power and that is the province of diesel. It is like a superpower arms race, only between the giants of locomotive manufacturing. In this case we're talking General Motors Electro-Motive Division and General Electric.

Now the first thing that novices want to know is why EMD and GE are dominant, and what's this talk of electro-motive. Many people don't understand that diesel engines are nothing but big generators powering electric traction units. This is where the contest for technological innovation and design improvement has been fiercest, and this is where competition has knocked off the other engine manufacturers.

It all started in the 1950s. Diesels had been around solidly for two decades, but now were taking over entirely. Here in the Midwest the reason was mostly the growing long-haul heavy load traffic. Diesels had already proven themselves in war to be handier switchers, and now it was clear that they were better suited to the task of unit trains and long trains of bulk freight.

EMD's F9 carbody locomotive and GP9 road-switcher were the big breakthroughs. Before that you had locomotive stalwarts Baldwin and Alco also building diesels as yard equipment or steel mill switchers. EMD upped the ante with its 16-cylinder, 1,750-horsepower units powering d.c. traction units. It was a new era.

Then in the 1960s, EMD stepped it up another notch by adding turbochargers to the diesels. This birthed the GP20 and SD24 and got others thinking. GE countered with its U25B, a 2,500-horsepower road-switcher. Alco tried to keep up, but folded in 1969. EMD put out the 2,000-horsepower GP38, the 3,000-horsepower SD40, and the 20-cylinder 3,600-horsepower SD45. GE followed with the 3,600-horsepower U36C.

The 1970s brought more innovations. Electrical systems benefited from space program developments. We on crews finally had direct contact with manufacturer design teams. The 1980s saw microprocessor controls come into use. GE brought out the DASH-8, a 4,000-horsepower breakthrough. In the 1990s EMD and GE both figured out how to replace the old d.c. traction technology with a.c. traction motors. This set the new standards at 5,000 and 6,000 horsepower for the big merged transcontinental railroads when they bought new units.

On the flip side you have the rise of the short lines. In a way they made the switchover to the new technology easier for the big boys. As the behemoths upgraded, the new short lines bought their old units. Some out west were still running Baldwins S-12s. EMD CF7s are making a comeback as a popular shortliner. Also RS-11s are around and will last forever. Not to mention all the EMD GP9s that will be handed down for years to come.

Then you have the switching and yard stuff. This was originally the birthplace of the diesel, and at one time the yards around Chicago had hundreds of switch engines. You had more manufacturers in this realm at one time. In addition to GE, EMD, Alco, and Baldwin, you had Fairbanks-Morse, Whitcomb, Porter, and Davenport all producing switchers in the 1940s and 1950s.

But over time the need for switchers declined. The shrinkage of the passenger train network was part of it. Switchers were the workhorses that moved passenger cars around the great terminals. Plus the thing that built demand for the big power units, the needs of intermodal and unit trains on long hauls, cut back the call for switchers. Freight by the carload became rarer, those small town lumberyards and feedmills were knocked off by the chains. Switching needs were now met by downgraded road engines. I heard that somebody was trying to build a new natural-gas-powered switcher, but I never heard if anything came of that.

If you had time, I could tell you about steam engines. I'm not an expert, but the men who trained me told me a thing or two about them.

RAILROAD BOOT CAMP

Many train buffs know of the historical context of military railroading in wartime. Some recall the combat feats of railroaders in the war zones. In times ranging from the Civil War up to World War II, such feats often evolved out of fate, with violent circumstances testing the mettle of ad hoc bands of railroaders. The results were often inspiring, if not downright heroic.

Truth be known, such rail skirmishes and operations were almost always emergency measures undertaken on short notice and seldom served any strategic vision. World War II planning placed military railroading on an entirely different footing, with years of calculation going into ways to turn German and Japanese rail systems against the Axis powers after invasions of occupied nations, island fortresses, and the enemy homelands themselves.

Rail operations were finally treated as integral parts of expeditionary forces, with the best available intelligence lent to the questions of how much rolling stock should be transported and how much of the enemy's could be seized or rehabilitated. Advance accounting penciled in amounts of replacement parts, ties, rails, fuel, tools, food for crews, medicine, and even prophylactics for bordello side trips.

Another aspect that was not left to chance in this modern round of combat railroading was the matter of training. In prior wars the railroader-at-arms, if he was lucky, might expect a brief interval of drilling and marching, followed by issuance of a weapon that real soldiers deemed antiquated. After that the chaos of war might well sweep him into such various and sundry tasks as guarding prisoners or manning gun emplacements.

In World War II the railroader was treated as a skilled resource. The experienced ones trained new recruits like Frank. Listen as he takes us back to railroad boot camp in his Minnesota backyard.

Most of us railroad "trainees" were sent to rail training after regular basic training. If you had much in the way of railroad experience you could wangle a transfer to a rail unit. That didn't always work for section men, who often were put in the bridge crews of the combat engineers. And the telegraphers and signalmen were often thrown into radio operator jobs.

So I was sent up from Mississippi to Fort Snelling, Minnesota. Being a Red Wing boy by birth and Great Northern man by blood, it was a heaven-sent assignment that ran directly against the military's usual talent for sending you as far away from home as possible to do things for which you lacked any aptitude. The fact that I overstated my railroad skill level had something to do with it. That and the army custom of throwing handy and willing bodies into vacant slots, never mind their bona fides.

Fort Snelling is where the 725th Railroad Operating Company instructed us in the standard operating procedures of military train operations. The program changed over its duration, with mixtures of military and civil railroad instructors. Experienced military railroad instructors were often snatched away and flown directly to staging areas, sometimes taken in the dead of night by Office of Strategic Services operatives for covert operations. When I was there we had classroom instruction from ancient officers reassigned from line units because of their girth and their waddles. The field instruction during my stay came courtesy of Omaha Railway crews down at St. James.

They were nice older men, too old for military service and more valuable to the home front anyway. We trainees with Milwaukee Road, Union Pacific, Santa Fe, Great Northern, and CNW ties gave them lots of ribbing about the Omaha line. I remember one Great Northern fellow from Montana who would drawl, "Come my first son, I'ma gonna give him the Omaha to set up under a Christmas tree."

But those Omaha fellows were good men and we could not have had better teachers for our short course in operating divisions. You learn more in a few months in that environment than you do in years of commercial railroading, because in a corporation everybody has turf they don't want your nose in. So we learned hand signals, how to spot cars, how to do light repairs on air hoses and brake shoes, and how to put a string of cars together.

We had the benefit of the accumulated wisdom of car foremen, section chiefs, trainmasters, roundhouse foremen, and experienced engineers. In order to "graduate" you had to know how to fire a steam locomotive, how to fuel a diesel, how to change a brass friction bearing, how to splice a telegraph line, and how to read maps and direct artillery fire.

We also accompanied them on various runs. We tagged along on little dinky way freights and extras. We went with them when they pulled the wrecking hook out to derailments and we learned how to limp damaged cars back to yards.

We had a good crew of trainees go through while I was there. Like me, a lot were young and brassy. Many were commissioned before the war was over and most ended up with management jobs with railroads. Most were army and headed for Europe, though we did train a few for other services. We had some Seabee or Navy Construction Battalion men and a few marines. I was in training with an Air Corps fellow who was destined to set up a rail operation in India to serve a huge airfield that was flying supplies over "the Hump" to China. After I went through I heard there were some Coast Guard men trained to set up port rail facilities.

I guess we weren't as fabled as some of those Southern Pacific men who formed the backbone of the early rail battalions and went in with invasion forces. But we were the second wave and did relieve a lot of those older men who didn't really belong in combat theaters. And we were as well prepared as one could be for such things.

Our old fossil military instructors knew that everything you learn can be out the window after the first shot. So they tried to simulate some combat conditions. And they sometimes got in trouble for it. Minnesotans did not like the live fire from overpasses, the smoke screens, the explosions off to the side of the right-of-way, or the low flying planes. But the whole point was to attune your eyes and ears to sights and sounds that you had to account for in addition to everything you have to worry about in normal train operations. The advice stood me in good stead as I remembered a suggestion to slow down if strafed from behind. It caused the enemy plane to overshoot us and before he could come around for a second run one of our fighters got him.

Listening to those old-timers was something. I wish someone had gotten their stories down. Many were World War I vets. They worked with the French railroads. It doesn't sound like American rail battalions were fully organized then. Some had extremely interesting experiences. One had helped seize railroads in Haiti and Nicaragua. One had commandeered Mexican trains in the border chases after Pancho Villa. Two were Spanish-American War vets, one in Cuba and one in the Philippines.

They taught us that military railroaders had to be self-reliant. Stories like the ones in France, where railroaders were issued antiquated .30-.40 Krag rifles and no ammo, struck home. We learned to swap to acquire machine guns, cooks, and medics. We learned that supply sergeants were God. We learned that a case of scotch delivered by rail to division headquarters kept generals ever mindful of our importance. We learned that permitting ease of transport to military police inclined these usually rigid personalities to be flexible in the release and return of wayward railroaders.

I didn't really get in the fray until late in the game. They loaned me to the Aussies and Brits fighting their way back up Malaya and Burma. So I got to piece together a hodgepodge of jungle fragments of different gauges. Usually we were behind the fighting, but there were still stragglers, snipers, and mines. We weren't as hands-on as the rail fellows in Europe; we had local crews to supervise.

I went from tech sergeant T-5 to second lieutenant to captain on waiver in less than a year. I should have never taken the captain's bars. I could have come home sooner instead of stamping rail requisition forms in Manila for six months. But it did move me up the railroad totem pole when I got back. The chestful of medals didn't hurt—bunch of stuff from the French, the Dutch, and the king of Siam. Got a Purple Heart too, though I was not hit by a bullet. The train took some sniper fire, I looked out the cab, the cowcatcher flipped up some sort of scrap, and a piece hit me.

But it all put me on the management track with the Great Northern. They forgot all about my meager experience of a few winters of clearing ice from switches and one summer as a fill-in hostler. My military railroad training had a lot to do with my surviving the Burlington Northern metamorphosis. So railroad boot camp was the best thing that ever happened to me.

PULLMAN HANKY-PANKY

Conductors on passenger trains are easily some of the best sources of railroad stories and some of the best storytellers. This should come as no surprise, considering the natural selection process that favors talkative and sociable individuals in their trade. They are far more likely to share anecdotes and train lore with the general public than other railroaders.

Many have great senses of humor and well-developed attitudes of live and let live. From the grandfatherly conductors of the bygone rural combination trains of coaches and freight to the polished professionals of Amtrak, conductors learn to deal with the foibles of passengers. Almost all can claim to have seen every variant of human behavior.

This is especially true of those conductors who worked the classic transcontinental passenger runs from the 1920s to the 1960s. While their numbers are dwindling, a few have sharp memories of rowdy and randy passengers. Bertram is in his ninth decade and doesn't get around very well. But he's willing to tell any visitors to his Chicago nursing home about the hijinks on sleeper trains.

I worked mostly on the Super Chief, the Chicago to Los Angeles train that set the standard for luxury train travel. I worked as a passenger conductor from 1939 to 1969. It was a good life and let me see things that I wouldn't have ordinarily seen in any other job.

Some railroad workers don't particularly like people. They think of the passengers as nuisances. They just as soon would haul potato bins or plywood as people. But I was always a people person. I love conversation and I've always been a joiner, from the Odd Fellows to the church choir. Older people from the grand age of passenger trains will often say to me, "Thanks for the memories." But I always come back, "No, thank you for the memories."

If you work the passenger trains long enough you see it all. All kinds of behavior and all kinds of human conditions. Laughs, tears, reunions, breakups, nastiness, compassion—you name it. If people are capable of a thing, then it's been done on a train.

In the grand age—I'm talking 1940s and 1950s—you could see the full range of the human race on the passenger trains. The homespun Ma and Pa Kettles with large broods of children in hand-me-downs and with their bountiful picnic baskets. The businessmen and salesmen with their briefcases and sample boxes. Not to mention the blue-blood ladies, the celebrities, the wealthy in private cars, the gangsters, the servicemen and servicewomen, and the honeymooners. I liked them all and made friends in each group.

Probably my favorites were those simple folk. Doesn't matter if they were hillbillies, Midwest hayseeds, or hardscrabble western ranchers. I could spot them as soon as they hit the platform. Big families, lots of bundles, roped together suitcases, rag dolls, baseball mitts, and those big picnic baskets I mentioned. Oh, the delights in those baskets! What I'd give for one of those sandwiches I remember: smokehouse ham on homemade bread with fresh grated horseradish. Let me tell you, an attentive conductor, one who put those kind of folks at ease, was likely to go home with a pint or two of homemade berry jam. Salt of the earth people! Where did they go? You don't hear about them anymore.

The businessmen and salesmen, they were like family in a way. Well, maybe more like neighbors, the train being our shared neighborhood. We saw them on a regular basis and we knew each other by name. Wasn't unusual for them to remember my children's names and I remembered many of their children's names. They weren't big tippers, but they were pretty liberal with free product samples, baseball tickets, free passes and vouchers. A pillow at the right time or holding a seat for them in a crowded club car might get you a weekend in a hotel they owned or a full course meal at a restaurant they had a deal with.

The blue bloods were a little stuck up at times. They usually wanted to be left in peace. But sometimes you'd see a wild streak in one of those old ladies, especially if she was traveling in a cross-country adventure with some grandchildren. I remember one who we helped by getting the kids to bed while she threw dice and drank shots with marines in a coach.

The GIs were something to see. So young in wartime! Mostly well-mannered young people. They still said "sir" and "ma'am" in those days. But you had to let them blow off a little steam on the train. Many had been stuck on military bases for long periods of time. Many were headed for places they might not come back from. If you saw a soldier and a Wac making eyes at each other, it was a good deed to find them a private spot. You wouldn't believe how many married couples told me that I got them together on the train that way. Makes up a little for me not going in the service myself.

You had to like those honeymooners. Mostly young first-timers to marriage. Usually city people who still didn't own automobiles, but who usually had a good union-wage job and could afford to splurge a little on a trip. Mostly, they just wanted their privacy. A good conductor made sure the porters and stewards didn't bother those couples too much. That, and rustling them up a bottle of champagne now and then. Though a few times I had to do some counseling about wedding night jitters.

At least the newlyweds had a sense of propriety. We had some travelers who ran toward the side of exhibitionism. You wouldn't believe how many times I saw hiked-up dresses on platforms between cars. Or how many times I had to break up a heated session in the rest rooms that was causing discomfort to other travelers.

What was amazing was how often these problems were caused by big shots or celebrities. Actors, singers, musicians, athletes—you name it. It wasn't like today where they think they can murder and get away with it. But they sure grew accustomed to people looking the other way at their hanky-panky. The real old-timers told me that as soon as trains had Pullman sleepers that all the problems of running a hotel moved right on the tracks.

Things I saw? How about a naked conga line of chorus girls going from car to car? How about strip poker with big-name baseball players and the gals from a class trip of a girls' college? How about a well-endowed actress popping them out of a tight dress in the dining car after too much wine? That's just for starters.

Those Hollywood boys were the wildest. Conductors swapped information about the real hell-raisers and it wasn't who you'd think. The Hollywood tough guys were mostly real gentlemen. Actors like Cagney, Robinson, and Bogart. It was those juvenile actors who were the biggest problems. Mickey Rooney was especially noted for chasing the girls around the train.

When those spoiled and overpaid kids were on the loose anything could happen in the compartments. Most people didn't even hear about pot until the hippies. But I smelled clouds of it on trains whenever we had those wild kids. That was usually along with the jazz musicians they brought on the trains or the high-class hookers. Along with those shenanigans there was the weird stuff—the threesomes, foursomes, and things I don't have names for.

The final category of passengers were the gangsters. They rarely caused problems for train crews or other passengers. When they did they were usually very apologetic about it and tipped us quite well to clean it up. Mostly their problems had to do with fights among themselves. On the other hand, they could be helpful if real trouble broke out. Once, at a derailment, some of our mafia passengers pulled out their guns and stopped the looting of injured people's belongings.

None of the things I mentioned were cause for reports to police. The railroad didn't want scandal. A troublesome drunk we'd put off the train. A little hanky-panky, well, we'd just look the other way.

TIMBER ROAD

Logging and other forest industries in the upper Midwest picked up steam when the railroads opened up the great pine woods. Previously limited by spring thaw movement of logs on streams and rivers, the arrival of trains in the north country accelerated the speed of cutting and shipment. There's no small irony in the current status of rail as "environmentally friendly" in light of the historical connection between the nineteenth-century arrival of tracks and the exploitation of resources on an industrial scale.

Rail transport also deepened the cycles of boom and bust in the remote areas by supplying the rest of the economy with raw materials. Railroads helped strip areas clean of trees, ore, and fuel. The railroad barons promised economic development and prosperity and instead became part of a process that turned thriving communities into ghost towns. The joke was often on the railroads as they struggled to maintain many miles of track in depressed regions. The term sustainable development *had not yet been coined and had it been in verbal currency it no doubt would have been lumped with pejoratives like* red *and* communist.

Despite the brief day of the timber short lines, they are fondly remembered. They have a secure place in the memories of a golden age of logging. Though many were narrow gauge and sputtered along with decrepit equipment, they were prized by north country residents as reliable four-season transportation in the land of wetlands, thick forest, and heavy snowfall.

Burt knows about such things only from his grandfather, a jack-of-all-trades on the Laona and Northern Railway in northeast Wisconsin. Now retired to his cottage near Argonne, Wisconsin, he has returned to his family's Forest County roots. He brings out the old photographs and brandy and soon it feels as if his grandfather is in the room.

Grandpop Roberts was born near Crandon sometime in the early 1880s. Very few white people up here back then, especially families. Just the beginning of logging, some trapping and foolish stump farming. It was a hard life, but they loved having their own patch of land. They all had independent streaks a yard wide.

Then the Laona and Northern came in 1902. Forest County was never the same. Grandpop Roberts said a place is done for once it's on the map and people know that there's a dollar to be made. But according to him, it was a good boom while it lasted. Made him enough money so his sons could learn trades and work in machine shops down in Milwaukee, which in turn meant his grandchildren could go to college. That's the American dream, right?

Grandpop helped build the railroad, starting with the tracks in the muck and brush. Told me he started at the bottom of the Laona and Northern and worked his way down. He said one of his first jobs was mosquito control using double-barreled shotguns and double-bit axes. After that he had to break black bears to harness to work as draft animals after the horses all died in the swamps. Along the way he had to serve as a guard and kill hostile hodags, hangdowns, hidebehinds, pumptifusels, gumberoos, and luferlangs.

He loved to regale little boys with such tall tales from the woods and from the railroad. Like his invention of "spring-loaded track," which he said you could roll out and roll up like a frisky carpet. He said it never caught on with the railroads though. So he sold the idea to all these small towns where they roll up the sidewalks after dark.

Seriously, he did love that railroad and he did just about every job on it, from water boy to supervisor. Naturally, his favorite position was locomotive engineer. He loved to operate the train and apparently was good at it. He said in the early days just about everybody got a turn at every job. And if you didn't hit anything, kill anybody, or dump the train off the tracks, you sort of came to be viewed as the official engineer.

Grandpop Roberts also had the reputation for using the train as a community service. He once prevented a big feud from turning violent when two family factions were headed toward each other in Laona. Put the train in between them and kept moving back and forth. Fortunately, they were too drunk and tired to walk around the ends of the train.

Another time he hauled a horse and rider down the line to throw a race for a local boy and against some sharpie in town to fleece the lumberjacks. That was a controversial move that earned him lifelong friends and permanent enemies. Guess it all depended on where they had placed their bets.

He was not above taking the locomotive out to bring a doctor to a hurt man at a lumber camp. Or to haul supplies out to stranded families. Or to pick up Potawatomi hunters with deer carcasses. He didn't go by schedules or regular stops. That's why they eventually made him a supervisor. They said he acted like he was in charge. But they didn't outsmart him. He continued to operate the locomotive even while in management.

Grandpop Roberts always said you couldn't stand on ceremony on a timber road. In his view, a railroad man in logging country had to be willing to pitch in on any job. He had to be fireman, brakeman, gandy dancer, you name it. Whatever it took to keep the train going and do what needed to be done.

He said they hauled their share of logs and would often help load. That's when men were killed, he said. They also hauled poles, hemlock bark, pulp cords, posts, and ties. Not to mention the occasional car of rock or gravel. Or the rare deluded farmer moving up from good ground to the south to the stone piles of Forest County. You can see some of that history at the Camp Five Logging Museum in Laona.

Grandpop Roberts always talked about "forking bark." As a boy, I misunderstood the words as obscene complaint about the trees. I came to understand that it meant loading hemlock bark with a pitchfork. The bark was destined for tanneries, I guess. I'm told hundreds of thousands of massive hemlocks were felled simply for the bark. They weren't viewed as a good timber tree.

That pains me. The hemlock is such a majestic tree. They grow slow and they need shade to get started. We'll never see stands like they cut.

You hear a story like that and in your gut you know that those old-timers were working more off muscle power than brain power. I don't condemn them. I only condemn us if we don't learn from it. Fellows like Grandpop Roberts were part of a brawny, heroic time. It makes for good stories. But we need to make sure we learn the right lessons.

Will we ever see another timber road? That's probably not the right question. We need to ask whether a railroad through the North Woods is appropriate for the communities and the forest. Thanks to Grandpop Roberts, I lean toward going slow on such things.

STEADY AS SHE GOES

Train crew stories are replete with special craft knowledge, wise mentoring, and heavy-handed engineers. It often occurred that engineers ruled over the steam era crews in ways comparable to feudal lords. The low man on the totem pole in this hierarchy was the fireman. Few firemen, despite their aspirations to ascend to engineer status, had anything positive to say about engineers.

Still, there was sometimes the man-to-man acknowledgment of skill and courage. Firemen of that time, consistent with the male code, rarely shared such sentiments with other train men. But a child or family member might be told an offhand account that hinted at respect and a vague bond.

These accounts often became family heirlooms, focused more on values than on rail lore. In the process, details about rail operations, places, and lines were lost. Some rail buff purists might insist that tales of this type were diluted past the point where they belong in a collection of railroad stories.

Don't tell that to the heir of this story. Steve is as proud of the fragments of this narrative as he is of the Omaha Railway, North Western, and Minneapolis and St. Louis Railway lanterns decorating his Stillwater, Minnesota, home.

He has a solid claim on the legacy by virtue of two railroading grandfathers and a baker's dozen of section crew uncles and cousins. A great-great-uncle passed on this tale.

The yarn came out of the Dahl family. It's fifty, sixty, maybe eighty years old. Where? That's a good question! Dahls were found on the railroads in Minnesota, Iowa, the Dakotas, and Nebraska. A couple harder-drinking Dahls even worked over in Wisconsin. Probably more German in their family trees than mine. But this story is supposed to come down from old Elmer, a hard-cussing great-uncle of my father.

Elmer spent most of his years on the Omaha line, west out of the Twin Cities. It was alleged, though never documented, that the old bugger did short youthful stints on the dirty goat road, the Great Northern, and America's repairful railroad, the Milwaukee Road. But you know how it is after a good trainman is sent Satan's way to stoke those big fires down below. The shiftless among the living will make up all manner of slurs and defamations. Other Dahls may have strayed from the Omaha in times of unemployment, but it's unlikely with old Elmer.

Elmer had one dream about railroading, one career goal. His focus was entirely on becoming an engineer on the Omaha and working the west end of that system. Like many with such a dream, he hoped to work up into this exalted status by serving his time as a collier at the hinges of hell, to wit, a fireman on a coal-burning, smoke-belching, whistle-tooting, steam-hissing locomotive on the old school midnight black and soot-encrusted engine and tender.

He never made it. Broke his heart, it did. Stayed a fireman until he was let go. Dad said Uncle Elmer did twenty or thirty years of that dirty bull work. He ended up a broken-down and crippled-up man. He had that forward apelike stoop of a perpetual shoveler. Some say that's how the rail bosses sorted out who made the grade. If you were gray at the temple but still ramrod straight in posture and natural complexion, then the rail gods might deem you fit to fondle the throttle. But, Lord forbid, would your knuckles start to drag on the tender deck, your face become cinder pocked, your hands grime encrusted, and your skin turned reptilian through the heat, well, you were done with engineer thoughts.

It was a caste system, pure and simple. Once a fireman was exposed as an evolutionary throwback, of Neanderthal blood, and lacking of Anglo Saxon credentials, how could he be entrusted with our grandest machines?

What fraternal order would permit a missing link into its gentlemanly ranks? Which enlightened management could allow its corporate image to suffer by permitting beasts to doff the cap to ladies and children from the exalted cab of the steam engine?

Elmer did not handle this situation well. He is remembered as a man governed by passions, an impatient man, a populist comfortable under both the black flag of anarchy and the red flag of insurrection. Once he knew that he would never ascend to the throttle, he came to hate engineers with every fiber of his stooped and sinewy body.

His hate was broad, deep, legendary, and almost mythic. The bile was sufficient to fuel a millennia-long campaign against Olympus, send Titans to the underworld, usher heroes into Valhalla, and empty heaven of angels. Yet it was barely sufficient to merit notice of a self-respecting engineer who, in professional courtesy befitting their station, made allowances for agitated firemen in recognition of their recent domestication as a species.

Suffice it to say that Elmer could talk railroading from sunrise to sunset on the day of the summer solstice and almost never utter a charitable word concerning an engineer. Stories about engineer heroism were sniffed at, their endurance ridiculed, their moral values mocked as fraud. He let it be known far and wide, and drummed into his blood relations as an absolute requirement of familial duty, that engineers were to be regarded as the living embodiment of humbuggery.

Such was the lore routinely dispensed at family reunions, in the moments of quiet when the rail men gathered for a covert pinch of tobacco out of sight of womanly disgust. Talk of Elmer, the railroad crew elite, and flim-flamming railroad bosses. It all fit neatly into our family's Farm-Labor sympathies, if not into our growing middle class and professional emergence.

I was easily into my fourteenth summer before I heard a variation in the story. It came up when the grown-up men talked about the need to keep one's head when the going got rough. It was as if there was a closely held male secret about how to maintain the presence of mind to deal with adversity. It was told with knowing nods and the whispered advice: "Steady as she goes."

The dirty family secret was that Elmer had learned this lesson from—heaven forbid—an engineer. And not just any engineer. No, Elmer's education in the stalwart and fearless arts came at the hands of Eddie "the Duke" Hill. Engineer Hill was thought of in those times as one of the most aristocratic, aloof, and antiseptic in a trade peopled by autocrats and anal personalities.

The Duke sported bowler hats, shirtsleeve garters, and natty vests as engine cab work clothes. The great unwashed of the manual railroad trades thought of him as a sissified bully.

Now, you can well imagine how it pained Elmer to credit such a creature with any backbone, intestinal fortitude, courage in extremis or any other manly quality. Mention of the Duke's service in the Spanish-American War and the Philippine Insurrection were derided with epithets such as "quartermaster" and "blanket clerk." Never mind that the real Boatswain Hill was remembered for passionless conduct in battle, engaged afloat in flimsy gunboats on murky Asian waters.

Old Elmer practically swore my elders to secrecy on how Duke saved a train. The telling and retelling of these tales must have been so hushed that many of the details were lost. I can't tell you where it happened, except somewhere west of St. Paul. Maybe down in the corner of the state. Can't even tell you the train number or even the line. The Duke shows up on different rosters at different times.

But the story has it that Elmer was pushing heat for the Duke on this run. Was it a bad rail joint or a spread in the track? No one knows for sure, but the engine trucks left the tracks at cruising speed. From an engine crew perspective this is one of the worst types of derailment, with no warning and no control. Nine times out of ten you'll get a tipover, especially on an embanked ballast.

A trainman doesn't know whether to jump, as with a looming collision that can be seen up ahead, or whether to ride it out. Either way had plenty of hazard. If you jump the wrong way, the engine could pull the cars over on top of you. If you hang in there, heavy loads behind you could put a long line of cars right up your rear end—heck, even up over the tender.

Elmer was fixing to jump in the direction opposite the engine's lean when the Duke gave him a glare. The engine had already begun its rodeo bucking as it clunked across ties, gnashing and splintering oak. The Duke showed no sign of doubt concerning the outcome. He stood rigid at the controls, yelling "Steady as she goes!"

It was the Duke's split-second thinking and skillful maneuver that gained Elmer's grudging admiration. The natural reaction would have been to throw the brakes. But the torque out of that action could have put the engine over on its side. So the dapper engineer performed a series of slight brake applications and alternated throttle speeds, feeling through the palms of his hands and the soles of his shoes the pressure of the train behind him, the bumps of the taking up of coupler slack, and light surges as the engine skidded across a few strong ties here and there.

On the engine careened, bumpty-bumpty on the ties, wheels screeching, sparks flying, and coupler knuckles clanging. Up and down galumphing while the shards of wood flew like hawks on the wind. One hundred feet at dangerous speed. Another hundred with the engine tottering this way then that. A couple hundred more feet with hundreds of tons of steel shuddering and groaning. Another hundred feet nice as a harness trotter at the county fair. And a final hundred feet walked up to a stop like a wounded soldier limping into an aid station. Through each phase and each control adjustment the Duke kept up the prayer: steady as she goes.

I guess Elmer really hated that haughty "of course I saved the train" look from the Duke. But I think it galled him even more that the Duke made it into train legend and he didn't. No fooling, the story became part of Minnesota railroad lore. First, as "the lost train" and then "the resurrected train" when it was reported missing and then found upright and intact. Second, as the Duke was feted as a master teamster and given a brass buggy whip with which to tame other engines. And third, as the embodiment of solid and fearless traincraft.

No fooling! You've heard the term Steady Eddie haven't you? Well, that's Eddie "the Duke" Hall, not Elmer Dahl.

ROLLING THE DISTANT SIGNAL

While railroads were never without their detractors, cases of train phobia and rail shyness were rare. Even in the days of predatory practices by rail conglomerates, the emotion most likely to be produced was anger, not aversion. A family with a rail history could often forgive (but not forget) union busting and thuggery in strikes, not to mention all sorts of economic heavy-handedness and flimflammery visited upon the community, and still romanticize the trains.

Many rail families treat their rail stories like treasured heirlooms, preserving them with reverence and pride. As for embellishments by subsequent generations, everyone excuses the careful polishing that goes into the care of any fine piece of craftsmanship. Though the family might affect an extremely proprietary air, as with any treasure, the satisfaction of possession is often linked to public knowledge of the inheritance.

A few rail families think otherwise. In such quarters there are sometimes secrets, skeletons in closets, and black sheep. Sometimes there is simply one bad experience that soured a family patriarch and left a brooding legacy for his descendants. Such is the story of Ned, a Cedar Rapids, Iowa, resident who made me aware that a railroad story could be a family's dirty laundry.

Always been a railroad fan, but a quiet one, from a distance knocked into me by the Old Man. He didn't mind the model railroading or the collector side of things. Just didn't want his sons around real live trains or trainmen. His sentiments weren't casual, being reinforced with a two-inch-wide leather belt applied to bare skin when our memories failed us.

It must have been an outlook beaten into him with even greater emphasis, though he never said so directly. We just knew that Grandpa Jack had told the Old Man to stay the hell away from railroads. It was a warning and threat underlined by venom and menace, made all the more intimidating by its utterance by a former railroad man who hardly spoke at all.

Grandpa Jack's railroad legacy was a hushed thing, a tale told in tiny fragments that only a decent puzzle jigger could piece together. Mention of it could get a boy's ear boxed, with persistence earning a quick trip to bed. Every family member knew that we were drenched in shame, painted with humiliation, and parboiled in the contempt of every God-fearing railroad family in Iowa and beyond. We were accursed unto the seventh generation.

As far as anyone could tell, this cloud over the family was from Grandpa Jack's days on the Fort Dodge line, though the particulars are lost in the mists of time and layered with many coats of family whitewash. A derailment was at the center of the story. Not your routine trucks-on-the-ties splinter whacker. Not your familiar pile of cars buried in the dirt. No, this one was a rip-snorting, rail-twisting, load-throwing, crew-jumping belly whomper. Type that turns a whole train into scrap and has a whole county talking about it three generations later.

Grandpa Jack was the fireman on this ill-fated train of doom. Legend pegs the engineer as one Nettleson, but that may be folklore driftwood washed up from the wake of another infamous Fort Dodge line wreck. The exact location is obscure too, the rumor placing it on a Fort Dodge inter-locking with another line. That would limit the sites somewhat and add to the confusion through some of the changes to Iowa interlockings with other lines in those days. The story is often placed "over in the hills."

The circumstances of the wreck are as muddled as you'd expect, but with a core of agreed-to facts. An interlocking switch was not fully turned. The switch flag was not properly displayed. This interlocking was notorious for bad visibility and had to be approached with care because of excessive angle and stopping distance. It was a site of earlier mishaps, so prudent crews were on notice.

But railroading often comes down to a game of minutes. Crews take pride in timeliness, and late trainmen are the goats of their lines. Not Grandpa Jack's gang. They took a chance and decided to roll that distant signal from a ways back, betting on it being in proper position.

They bet wrong. The switch point was closed just enough to catch the lead trucks and flip them sideways. From that point on, the law of physics took over. Drive wheels tore the switch and a goodly portion of track clean out of the ground. The tender took a bullfrog hop and launched coal into space—it still falls to Earth as shooting stars. Behind are twenty-five cars eager to join the fun if they can fight their way through the ties set upright like fence posts and rails swinging like angry hammers.

I'm told that such an event can be a noisy affair, with groans of metal, clanging, banging, and odd sounds that you wouldn't expect. Some talk about whizzing and whining like on a battlefield, about pieces of metal singing by like bullets and shrapnel. Some talk about whooshing air and loud cracks, often the result of rails turned into missiles that can go straight through a freight car like armor piercing artillery shells. Then there are the strange whistles of couplers flung skyward, screeches of steel tearing like paper, the grinding of iron, the cracking of loads, and the full church organ of brake line pipes, brake beams, locked brake shoes, and hissing air.

Those who've been through a derailment say that it can be over-whelming in sights and sensations. Some report a vibration on the order of an earthquake, some an abrupt jolt and slam like an auto wreck. I've heard talk of slow motion or stop-action time experiences. Others report surreal images of boxcars soaring overhead and immense furrows cut into the ground.

These things must have assaulted Grandpa Jack's senses, if he wasn't hiding his head somewhere. That natural reaction being a distinct possibility in this case, seeing how he is reported to have bailed out as they ran the switch point. Except for the engineer, they all jumped. Not a safe thing in itself and advisable only under some collapsed bridge and levee conditions or an impending head-on collision. Otherwise it suggests panic and a disregard for the likelihood of being run over by the rest of your train. You jump from cabooses, and then only if you're not getting rear-ended.

The engineer rode her down. Not that it did him any good. The entire crew was given the boot, a harsh judgment given their extensive injuries. It was thought that there would have been less disgrace in death, survival in this case proving how unlucky those men were and how removal from the society of true blue railmen was foreordained by higher powers.

Their lives after that were to be dominated by recriminations, finger pointing, and attempts to live with shame. This was the family legacy and the reason for the Old Man's admonishments. The Old Man would roll in his grave if he knew my brother, Bud, and I re-create that wreck for the grandchildren on the model layout in the basement.

UNDERCOVER ENGINE TRAINEE

Concealed identity is a theme in older railroad stories, especially those from the Great Rail Strike of 1877 and the later turmoil involving the Industrial Workers of the World. Railroad workers fleeing trumped-up indictments delivered by management-friendly courts found it wise to ply their craft under different names. This was most common among foreign-born union activists subject to deportation.

Subterfuge is a long and proud tradition in a country where people came explicitly to reinvent themselves. Many an old American family treasures legends of ancestors who poached the king's game, or stole a horse or even a kiss from a royal-born maid, and hence fled to the New World with nom de voyage.

Americans also treasure certain gender disguises. Until the modern era of medical examinations as a routine part of military induction, every American war had stories of women as covert comrades in arms. World War II's necessities challenged gender roles openly and brought women into a host of occupations. Still, just like the barrier between support roles and combat arms in the military, some parts of industrial life remained closed to women despite wartime needs. Railroad crews were one of those areas.

That didn't stop Evelyn, a spunky young farm girl from south central Iowa. Every male in her family had done a turn at railroad work. Her grandfathers had graded right-of-ways up from Missouri with horse teams. Her father was a brakeman until an accident took some fingers. Her brothers, all drafted into World War II, alternated farm work and track work on the Milwaukee Road, Burlington, and Chicago Great Western. She insists that details be kept vague to protect the guilty.

I was young, kind of a tomboy given to wearing overalls. They just thought I was a boy when I was hanging around the yard. So when they needed help as the war got going it was just natural they asked me.

Dad always called me Evan anyway. That's what they knew me as down at the yard. Dad knew I started to work on the railroad, but he thought I cleaned the depot. Mom kept the secret and Dad never checked 'cause it was too hard on him to be around the train. Every whistle made him feel for his missing fingers.

I started in the roundhouse. Put in two full years in a washing stall. Had enough scrubbing for a lifetime. Talk about rough and cracked hands. It was a dirty job, but Mom and Dad were glad for the money.

It was a job that women were doing on other places on the railroads, so it wasn't really that big of a deal to be working in the roundhouse. And I guess at that stage I didn't look at it as deception. I never said I was a man and no one in the roundhouse ever asked. They just thought me a bit odd and shy for not sharing their public toilet habits.

I was something of a pet around the rail operation. To them I was this beardless energetic boy who wanted to learn everything. I clerked for a year or so after the washing stalls. Then I helped the hostlers and found my true love moving locomotives.

This was when diesel was coming in. We started to see them pulling war freight. Then a small switch engine came to the yard. Finally they announced a new program for engine trainees. Someone suggested I put my name in for the training. I did so, partly as a lark. I never thought I would be picked. Wouldn't they see me as a skinny kid with a raggedy mop of hair? I guess not.

When my name came up I didn't know what to do. Mom urged me forward, taking secret delight in what I was getting away with. Then again, she was always open to a promotion which brought a bigger paycheck into the house. So, after some indecision, I decided to give it a try. What did I have to lose? As it turned out, my job.

Being an engine trainee started off well enough. They were pretty nice to us. Told us how we were going to be the leaders of the new diesel era. The engineers who trained us were a bit crusty, but at least they themselves had adapted from steam to diesel. Some engineers took satisfaction that the trainees were drawn from a pool of bright young employees, not from the ranks of disgruntled firemen or brakemen. It seemed to tickle their sense of being the elite of the railroad and satisfy their sense that they could make over the railroad in their image without the bad habits of others creeping in.

The early phases of the training were about signals operating instructions, and safety. Then we started to do these "ride alongs." In the beginning all I was supposed to do was watch, stay out of the way, and keep my mouth shut. After a bit, they would give me little tasks or ask me to step up and read a gauge or look back on a curve for hotboxes or rocking side bearings.

It all fell apart for me when I switched over to another crew. They put us in brand new F-3 locomotives, an A and a B unit shiny as a new suit. I met the crew on the ready track between the old coal tower and the depot. I was told to keep my eyes peeled as a yard switchman sent us east to the main track. All the while the engineer was quizzing me on what I knew, what I've done.

He seemed pleased with my answers and my pedigree. He gave me a wink when he told me to get off with the engine brakeman to get us set up on the waiting track, even though the brakeman gave him a dirty look. The engineer was a good-looking thirty-five-year-old man, which made him the youngest engineer I had seen by at least three decades. He was a medically discharged fighter pilot. He was the first railroad worker I saw as anything other than a greasy pear-shaped male in coveralls. Maybe I looked at him in a way that betrayed me, as the engine backed through the switch.

The front brakeman coupled up with a curse at stiff pin lifters. Then we built up pressure and ran an air test and walking inspection. Back at the caboose, the rear brakeman gave us the ready sign. The handsome engineer released the air and the front brakeman and I swung up on the F-3s. In the cab again, the engineer gave me another wink.

He started quizzing me again. What did I see in the yard? Did I notice the flagged track with the tank cars under repair? How many carmen did I see working there? Did I see their tools lying on an adjacent track? How many work trucks did I see up toward the roundhouse? Could I tell what they were working on?

He summoned me closer in the cab as the noise of the F-3 started to rise. He told me that there were two basic types of operating dangers. He called them yard dangers and main-line dangers. Yard dangers came from poor visibility and too many railroad people, who should know better, getting in the way. Main-line dangers came from stupidity and acts of God. He said a young man racing a train to see if an old roadster could make it to a crossing first could be chalked up to stupidity. On the other hand, a shed blown on the tracks by a storm was an act of God. He also joked that anytime a farmer or his livestock ended up on the tracks it was part act of God and part stupidity.

He asked me to move closer, asked me to feel the tension on his foot that was on the emergency pedal, asked me to feel the vibration in his hand wrapped on the throttle. He told me to move the throttle into the second position. We crept ahead. I turned with the front brakeman to watch the rear brakeman close switches behind us and jump on the caboose. The engineer had me move the throttle up through the positions as we cleared the yard. After we passed a passenger train he put his hand over mine as we moved the throttle to position eight.

The loud hum kept conversation to a minimum, but he gave me a look of shared pleasure. It was as if he was asking with his eyes: doesn't that feel good. It was in that moment that my railroad future unraveled. He brushed by me a little too closely in the close quarters of the cab. "You're a woman, aren't you?" he yelled.

- Didn't say another word to me the rest of the trip. When we were done, he gave me a disgusted look and said he didn't like to be fooled. He made me resign from the railroad, quietly and without scandal. We talked privately about that day about once a year for many years. Then at our fiftieth wedding anniversary he told the whole story to our children, grandchildren, and great-grandchildren. If you think they were surprised, you should have seen the look on the Amtrak conductor's face when my husband told him the same story a week later on the way to New Orleans.

"EASTERNERS"

Heartland railroad lore inevitably hints at connections to the Great Plains, the Pacific, and Canada. Midwest railroads seem to knit together two-thirds of the country. Oddly enough, this regional consciousness does not extend eastward into well-established rail connections. Perhaps if the Illinois Central had lines to the Atlantic instead of the Gulf of Mexico or if the Milwaukee Road's Hiawatha had connected to New York there might have been some deeper tie to the East.

In some heartland railroad circles there were dismissive attitudes toward the "easterners," despite their high ranking among the classic lines. Midwestern railroaders had little regard for the coastal giants like Baltimore & Ohio, Pennsylvania, and New York Central. They had even less respect for the patched together successors like Conrail and CSX, heir to the Chessie System.

But, more than a few employees of the eastern lines were right here in the Midwest. Their story was not commonly told after the cessation of the premier passenger trains out of New York and Washington, D.C., that connected to Chicago, Detroit, and St. Louis. Only heirs to the legacy talk about it anymore.

Rowley finished out his railroad time with the Milwaukee Road and the Soo at Savanna, Illinois, and still resides in an apartment there. But his fondest memories flow from time at the engine throttle in places like Toledo, Ohio, and Gary, Indiana. Listen in on an heirloom tale.

At BLE conventions the Chicagoans called us "easterners" and attached the term to various ethnic slurs that circulated in the Brotherhood of Locomotive Engineers in those days. This was even though they knew we were Midwesterners of the same stock they were. It was just a dislike of anything or anybody connected to New York. This always had those of us on the Baltimore & Ohio, which was a real border state line, scratching our heads.

I started on the B&O in the mid-1960s. Things had just started to turn around with the rise of the unit coal trains. An arrangement with the Chesapeake & Ohio improved our whole operation. By 1973, the B&O, the C&O, and the Western Maryland were all subsidiaries of the Chessie System. This was good for operations, but not so good for some of us with slight seniority. So it was time for me to move on.

But I kept up with news of the easterners whenever I got home to La Paz, Indiana. Our whole clan was connected to eastern lines. Pop and the uncles were all B&O. That's how I got on. But some of the cousins and in-laws worked the Pennsylvania Railroad and the New York Central. And we had a few black sheep with Indiana Harbor Belt Railroad and operating switchers in the Gary steel mills.

The debate around the table always came down to the Broadway Limited versus the Twentieth Century Limited versus the Capitol Limited. These were the crack passenger runs of the eastern lines into Chicago. We had men in our extended family who had been engineers on all three, so there was quite a bit of pride and competition. Pop and his circle were naturally inclined toward B&O's Capitol Limited. The Cap was the all-sleeping-car overnight train. It had excellent club and dining facilities.

As far as I know, it was the first passenger train to show feature movies in club cars. They also pointed out that B&O was the only eastern line to run dome cars, which was sure nice for the views in the Ohio Valley and the Allegheny Mountains. They had pride in the B&O up until the day in 1987 it was dissolved and totally absorbed into CSX.

The Cap would arrive after dawn in Chicago, except in winter. It came in south of Chicago's Loop and then backed into Grand Central Station, not to be confused with New York's Grand Central Terminal. It was a real VIP train. Pop said it was not unusual for senators, cabinet secretaries, and ambassadors to ask to ride up in the engine cab. He also said that there was hardly a Cap engineer who didn't have a snapshot taken with the likes of Betty Grable or Rita Hayworth.

The Columbian was the sister train of the Cap. It was an all-coach train, no sleepers, so it didn't have the prestige or the ritzy crowd of the Cap. But it was also a mighty fine train. Both trains went diesel electric very early, much to the chagrin of all the coal mines served by the B&O.

Now with some of the cousins, the New York Central came up at the kitchen table. In the late 1960s two brothers in one family were criss-crossing each other east of Chicago. One was engineer of the Twilight Limited, the streamliner on the afternoon run from Chicago to Detroit. The other was engineer on the last stretch of the Chicagoan, one of the Central's New York–to-Chicago passenger trains. Some of the other famed New York connections were the Commodore Vanderbilt, the Lake Shore Limited, the Peacemaker, and the Twentieth Century Limited. There was also the Wolverine, to New York via Detroit, and the New England States, which crossed upstate New York on the way to Boston.

Family consensus had it that the Twentieth Century Limited was the Central's crack run. It made the New York–to-Chicago trip in around fifteen and a half hours. It's true that New York high society and foreign dignitaries preferred the Century. It was a matter of custom-made dishes and glassware, Art Deco design, actual red carpet rolled out at boarding, and the best martinis that could be sipped at 100 miles per hour. Problem was, it was so snooty a regular person couldn't get on it. You had to know a Rockefeller to make a reservation. But it was a sight to see as it pulled into the La Salle Street Station.

Our partisans of the Central gloated about how their line was better positioned than the B&O. They always got a kick out of B&O's financial woes. The Central had the good fortune to avoid the worst of the Appalachians and the Ohio Valley floodplains. That saved millions of dollars every year. Not to mention its dominant position in New England, with good connections in Quebec, Ontario, and Michigan.

Now, the Pennsylvania, that was a different breed of cat. The Pennsy was a country onto itself. It was like the railroad was an afterthought to its commercial empire. They owned foundries, roller mills, fabrication shops, coal mines, dams, power plants, grain elevators, natural gas fields, hotels, ships, ferries, and telephone systems. In its prime it was a 28,000-mile system.

It was nothing to sneeze at, though of suspect reputation among rail-roaders. It was the type of system that the Milwaukee Road and Great Northern aspired to be. The Pennsy held the controlling interest in distin-guished lines like the Wabash and the Norfolk & Western. They built their own equipment, engines, rolling stock, docks, and terminals. But they bled themselves white competing with the Central and trying to drive the B&O under. They were cutthroats, and we had a good laugh when they were sucked into the Penn Central merger. Even a bigger laugh as infighting in the merged road brought about bankruptcy and the indignity of Conrail's guardianship.

But they did have a premier run like the other eastern lines. In Pennsy's case it was the Broadway Limited, the all-private-room train on the New York–to–Chicago route. It was not the celebrity train like the Cap. It was not the snob train like the Century. But it was clearly the domain of the prosperous businessman. Especially the well-fed businessman. One of the few trains with twin car diners, it was famed for food. I have heard former passengers lovingly describe the roast duck 'a la orange and the lobster thermidor like it was yesterday. It was the only train I know of where stewards brought some of that great eating up into the engine. That's according to some of the in-laws who worked a few turns.

Most of the Pennsy relatives ran freight to Wabash interchanges or worked the Kentuckian to Louisville. But they were loyal, just like the rest of us were to our lines. It was a friendly competition among friends and extended family. We were all proud to be "easterners" railroading in the Midwest.

WRECK OF THE *MILWAUKEE*

Tragedy is never far from the thoughts of heartland railroaders. Derailments, crossing accidents, and the ravages of cold steel upon skin and bone shape memories and conduct. But generations of north country railworkers have accepted the hazards as part of the territory.

Railroaders nod their caps in respect to other dangerous crafts. More than one family began their rail association because a patriarch warned of death and disability in the mines, the logging camps, and the Great Lakes. Few in the rail crafts, however, concede much to other occupations in terms of dangers or rigors.

It is a rare trainman who has a story that hints at the travails of other occupations. It is just not in their nature or accepted ritual in their subculture. Expressions of blue-collar solidarity are generally hard to find. Where they are found is in the places where rail links to other work: the timber regions, the ore lines, and, most of all in our area, the port docks.

Below is the only story I found in which a trainman glorified and memorialized another mode of transportation. Roderick is a frustrated ship's master who never left dry ground. But he spent a work life with the smell of Lake Michigan in his nose and the cries of the gulls in his ears. Sit down with him on the bench outside of the Maritime Museum at Manitowoc, Wisconsin.

Our family sent many men down to the lake in boats. That was the clan's trade back in Holland. But the North Sea and Channel in the old country never took the toll claimed by those angry mistresses called Michigan, Huron, and Superior. Don't know of a Dutch Reformed church within sight of the lakes that doesn't have a ledger with entries summed up as "lost on the lake." We lost a baker's dozen just in our family. That's why Dad told me to stay off the lakes and get a railroad job.

I followed his advice, worked my way up in train crews until I learned to operate diesels, and headed straight to switch crews near the docks. Worked in Milwaukee and Green Bay for the Chicago & North Western. Then I got my chance to come home to Manitowoc and work the CNW connection to the C&O coal ferries. Right into the best job in the best rig, loading and unloading ferries with an Alco S#2 switch engine. Best switcher ever made in my view.

It was a job I wanted and one that I was prepared for by blood. I never moved a freight car off or on a ferry without Dad's story of the *Milwaukee* ringing in my ears, or without the old faded postcard of the big car ferry stuck up in the switcher cab. You don't know the story? You call yourself a story collector? Holy diesel fuel! It's just one of the most horrible Great Lakes disasters on record.

You young pups get all teary about the *Edmund Fitzgerald*. Play that weepy song on the jukebox, drink your beer, and yank your crank. Well, let me tell you, those whippersnappers on the "Ed Fitz" went down cleaner and less painfully than the *Milwaukee*.

The fateful night of mountainous seas was October 22, 1929. A night as wild as anything ever recorded on the Great Lakes. Towering waves washed away lighthouses, destroyed docks, and sheared thousands of rivets in steel-hulled ships. Out on the lake, wise captains turned north-ward into the waves. But not Captain Robert "Heavyweather" McKay. He had a reputation for going out under all circumstances, and the ferry line was noted for prodding captains to stay on schedule.

The *Milwaukee* carried a cargo of twenty-five railroad cars bound for

Michigan, where they would connect with the Grand Trunk Western. Grand Trunk's ferries were the only vessels to leave port during that stormy night. They had the arrogance that went with their heavy-duty year-round equipment. They ran in winter conditions akin to arctic navigation. So what was a storm?

Lots of rumors popped to the surface with the *Milwaukee's* wreckage. Defective sea gate on the stern. Weak bulkhead below the car deck. Bad hatches on the after spaces. But the whispers that haunted railroaders had to do with bad loading procedure and improper securing of the cars.

The loads included cars of lumber, feed, canned peas, grain, bathtubs, butter, cheese, and automobiles. There was some talk that the foul weather hurried the loading process and put too much weight in the stern. The dockside crew wanted to get out of the lashing rain and had no expectation that the *Milwaukee* would leave under these circumstances. Some say that the predeparture checklist was not followed because they fully expected to recheck the chains and latches after the storm. Some say that the whole dockside crew was shocked when McKay blew the whistle and cast off the hawsers.

The federal inspectors said that the car ferry was structurally sound. But a picture emerged of that terrible night which pointed to a combination of human folly, load shifts, and equipment failure under huge distress. The Coast Guard light boat east of Milwaukee noted McKay holding due east, pitching and rolling, instead of a prudent northeast course to meet the waves and troughs. Old mariners think she started to fill herself over the stern and that stubborn McKay finally swung around. That's when the sea gate was probably carried away. Shoddy fasteners at this point would have been fatal. Imagine a pitching deck with loose freight cars. It would take only a bit of that pounding to buckle plates, pop rivets, and breech the watertight integrity of the vessels. That done, a few more waves over the stern probably set her to the bottom like a rock.

Just imagine the hell in those minutes. Deckhands struggling to secure cars, dodging loads, and getting crushed or swept overboard by them. Men below in crew compartments inundated and trapped. Enginemen tossed and buried by shifting coal in the boiler room. Muscle and adrenaline thrown into battle against cold steel and frigid water. Then the quick end, slipping beneath the waves to a watery grave.

So back to those docks and ferry switches that occupied my CNW days. Nothing like the thought of those last car-thrashing minutes on the *Milwaukee* to focus mind while loading rolling stock. Kind of makes a fellow think that he's arming a bomb. Everybody kind of watches each other. Every move is triple-checked. I know I got on the nerves of some, asking again and again if we were spotted correctly or if the front cars were secure. For this they sometimes called me "Granny," even on the Soo docks and the Pere Marquette crews.

But I "worked the apron" as smooth as a surgeon. The apron is the flexible portion of the dock that connects the tracks on land to the tracks on the ferry. The apron rises and falls with the ferry, whether by wave action or the gradual displacement of water by the weight of cars. Working the apron is an art that developed over time; supposedly the first engine to work a car ferry pushed the ferry away from the dock and fell in the drink.

The solution to that little problem was to use idler flats, empty cars placed between the loads and the switcher. The way this works is that the idler flats are what moves back and forth on the apron. They're light and allow for flexing. We used short maintenance-of-way size flats, not the new long ones that you see hauling structural steel.

On the ferry, the crew "dogs down" the cars. The "dogs" are a wedge-locking device to immobilize the cars. Over time there were chain jack fasterners and bolt chocks. There were lots of innovations brought about by bad experiences with simple wheel chocks. The early problems with loose cars smashing right through the bottom of ferries was a problem that demanded mechanical solution.

In our day working the ferries, everyone knew the stakes. Everything had to be just right. Our family was spread out from Racine to Sturgeon Bay, clustered in Sheboygan and Manitowoc and filled with kitchen stories of great-uncles on packet ships and great-grandfathers on fishing boats. All lives lost on the lakes were remembered in reverent whispers at those kitchen tables. But none more so than the forty-seven souls, six of our blood, that went down with the *Milwaukee*.

PART TWO
Grease, Cinders, and Signals

Little glamour is found in the maintenance and technical trades, though they are indispensable to the operation of any railroad. Much of the maintenance work is hard, dirty, and monotonous. Much of the technical work is categorized by isolation, strange hours, and split-second judgment. These are the tales of back-breaking work, friction with train crews, danger, injury, and death. Despite the stress, grime, and blood, a strong work ethic and sense of accomplishment are evident throughout these tales.

STEAMED UP

While the number of steam locomotive fans seems to increase with each passing year, the select circle of those on intimate mechanical terms with the old-time power units has dwindled to a handful of preservationists and aged tradesmen. They will tell you that once upon a time there were those on the Earth who could diagnose an engine's malady by ear, at some miles' distance. They speak, almost mythically, about a subbreed of men who could claim descent from the earliest smoke-grimed tenders of forges and workers of metal.

Is it not, they ask, a magical talent bestowed by gods to be able to take rock and replicate Vulcan's fire in order to liquify, purify, and mold? In their question is the hint of uncertainty about whether the patron deities of such skill reside in heaven or in parts far below.

Romantic as the image of engineer (he of clean overalls and cap and fiery bandanna about the neck) might be, there are those who revere the builders and tenders of the great steam engines as the true priests of the old-time religion. In such quarters the boilermakers of the manufacturers' foundries and the railroads' locomotive shops are seen as the last humans privileged to possess the mystic secrets of harnessing elemental forces and materials in ways simple and sublime.

Stefan is one such disciple. He clings to the memories of his youthful years in the locomotive shops as stubbornly as he does to his residence in a tough South Side Chicago neighborhood and to his ancestors' Eastern Europe habits. Don't tell him the days of steam are over. For him it is just a lull.

Steam will come back, one way or another. People don't realize that it never really went away. I spent over forty years working with steam, from the locomotive shops to nuclear reactors. Steam is out of view now, hidden in power plants and underground tunnels, making electricity and providing heat. But a boy gets no chance to see its power like in the days when he might stand on a train platform and have an engineer tease him with a leak or a blast.

I started in the Fortieth Street Shops in Chicago soon after World War II. My father said, Stefan, you go learn a trade with that Chicago & North Western Railroad, that will be a good long job for your life. His predictions were about as bad as his English. He and my mother came out of those European people pushed around for hundreds of years, part Polish, part Bohemian, and maybe even Hungarian. This was the poor man who welcomed the German army and for his reward he gave them five years' slave labor in steel mills and railroad shops.

But it was from him that I knew metal. Further back the family were tinsmiths. So we have it in the blood to make metal do what it doesn't want to do. Metal does not want to bend, take on a pleasing shape, or do anything useful. You have to tame it and out-trick it.

Those old-time boilermakers, locomotive machinists, and shop mechanics, now, they knew the tricks. I only worked with them a few years before it was easy to see that steam was ending on the railroad. But eh, what they taught me to look for, listen to, feel through the fingertips, and smell. Some could taste a metal residue and tell you about wear deep inside the locomotive. A few even had a sixth sense that went right to the heart of those black beasts.

As a rule, men in the shops had good hearing. This is no small thing when you think about the background sound. The heavy pounding, the grinding, and the loud noises of every type. To work twenty or thirty years in the locomotive shops, in days before ear protection, and have any hearing at all is a miracle. But the things these men could hear. They could pick up the smallest sounds in a bearing or piston that told of wear or alignment problems. In the sound of hiss and steam they knew by instinct how the pressure must be adjusted.

Sometimes it was the total senses and their knowledge of the railroad. They would listen, taste the calcium scaling in the pipes, look at the wear marks. Then they might say, this one's been in hard mine service, working steep grades, drawing bad water, and pulling overloads. They were like good doctors.

In the Fortieth Street Shops we did the heaviest repairs. If we couldn't do it, well then it was a total manufacturer refit or the scrap pile. Usually the scrap pile. We did mostly the Class 1 and 2 repairs, the major boiler and pipe work. We got the bad stuff from the whole CNW system. In Clinton they did lighter boiler cleaning and some drive wheel work.

We did much of the heavy work with overhead cranes. These were the most powerful machines I had seen in my life up to that point. With them we could move large parts and equipment very quickly. It was almost like an assembly line in there.

It was all teamwork. A boilermaker and his apprentice didn't work alone. We talked with the machinists, the welders, the pipefitters, even the electricians and the laborers. Never since have I seen men work so good together. Maybe because diesel was coming and breathing down their necks. Maybe because they learned their trades the old way and nothing was to leave that shop unless it was fixed right. The old men said we want crews to think that a locomotive out of the Fortieth Street Shops is as good as the best to roll out of Baldwin's locomotive works in their glory days. That's how they talked about it, because to the old men Baldwin was the Cadillac of locomotives.

From men such as these you could learn many things. Things that are now lost arts. How to heat and handle a rivet. Some would turn them so gently, to evenly heat them and so as to not nick them in the slightest way. How to prepare metal for brazing or welding, getting the cleanest possible surface. How to pick out the best metal stock for the job and send the rest to the car shops.

Knowing metal was the key. These men knew the history of iron and steel. They knew the quality of the ore sources. They knew the competence of mills and foundries. They knew the impurities of the fuels used by each manufacturer. They talked about lessons learned a hundred years before in Pittsburgh. They expected a glorious future, with more technology ahead for locomotives.

It makes a man wonder. How did it all change so fast? We have much more coal than diesel fuel. It has to come back, doesn't it? I get hot under the collar just thinking about what we lost. Internal combustion is not something that will help us in the long haul. Steam is more natural.

EPITAPH FOR A SECTION HAND

No full accounting exists of the lives lost while laying or maintaining track. If the tally were to include a continent-wide book of the railroad construction dead, especially if the losses from the mountain tunnel bores and the deep valley trestles were thrown in, then the list would be grimly impressive. The casualty roster would be on the scale of some of our wars.

Yet one does not see memorials in town squares erected in recognition of gandy dancers or bridge crews. Railroad commemoration days are not set and marked by bombastic political speeches. Yet few stretches of track are without their fallen. For many communities the sacrifice of lives in the course of connecting them to the outside world had a far more tangible meaning than heroics in banana republics.

In the Great Middle of America, death on the tracks came on the variously shod feet of grim reapers of cold, heat, fire, and a host of accidental causes. Section men have been crushed, decapitated, disemboweled, impaled, buried alive, and severed in two. Some were interred at the site of their demise, others boxed and shipped to faraway places. More than a few left no identity beyond their payroll "x"; others left large broods of orphans to mourn them.

Here and there a family might keep a treasured old photo and tend a grave of a section man killed out on the line. Rail town historical societies might preserve a file of newspaper clippings and artifacts. But, by and large, these dead are forgotten.

Not so in one Madelia, Minnesota, family. There the discreet might be invited to a private shrine. It is one of those oddities that can be found here and there across America: a combination of religious grotto and kitschy patio lounge. It's Irma's backyard, passed down by virtue of hereditary title from railroaders long gone. Let her give you the tour.

This flower box is from ties taken from the fatal siding. Later than the accident, of course. The edging is entirely of railroad spikes, thousands of them. The cross is made of crossing sign posts. That's why the STOP–LOOK–LISTEN thingamajig is still on it. It's not meant as a religious warning, though some people take it that way.

My Jesus is standing in a steel railroad signal box. It really helps keep his colors from fading. Those trinkets around his neck are switch keys. His area is set off by a square marked by four switch stands.

Along the fence we have the placards of many railroads. People bring them here for good luck. Look at some of those old ones: Erie-Lackawanna, Frisco Line, Boston and Main, Seaboard Coast Line, Fort Dodge, Green Bay and Western. They leave them for good luck, they leave them in memory of men lost on those lines, and they leave them for reasons they don't begin to understand.

It's that way about how they get here. They're only a few in number during the summer months. They always ask quite politely and say they heard about the Case Memorial from a friend. It's never anybody I've heard of, but they look harmless enough. Some try to leave money, others want me to put a sign out, but I'm content to sit in my fenced backyard.

My late husband welded together that scale model of a locomotive and tender out of tie plates. His father chiseled the inscription in the marker stone. A nephew painted the mural on the fence. Together they tell the story of Shorty Case.

Shorty Case was an Omaha Line section man. He had some local family, but it was said that they were not close. Many unkind things were apparently said about the man while he lived and for a time after his death. They made sport of his stature and his fate.

Things were said like, "Here's a matchbox for his coffin," and "If you're a small man, even a little carelessness can kill you." There was quite a bit of mean-spiritedness going about. The greater measure of jocularity resulted from the precise nature of the accident.

Shorty and the crew were working right here at Madelia. They were taking their lunch break by the end of a boxcar. Shorty was sitting right on the rail near the coupler. The switch to that siding was supposed to be closed and the foreman had sent someone to peer around the cars to check the switch stand semaphores. It looked closed from that angle. Well, it looked closed from the angle of a freight train pulling through the yard. The switch stand had a bolt missing and a strange twist to it. So the engineer mistakenly ran the switch and struck the boxcar.

It took half a day to get Shorty out from under there. They say much of his body had the look of tenderized swiss steak. More to the point, they say he lived several hours and talked as if he felt little pain. Some said that he asked to be fed the rest of his sandwich. So it was called a "short lunch break," "sandwich from a short order cook," things like that.

That's why the stone reads as follows:

In Memory of Shorty Case
He lived a short life
He ate a short lunch
Before he was done
He was shorter by a bunch.

HIGH ALTITUDE RAILROADING

Few remember a time when railroading was thought of the same way as maritime activity or aviation without radar or instruments. Such situations require lookouts. In areas of railroad density the men perched above yards and interchanges were indispensable to life, limb, and profit margin.

Like modern day air traffic controllers, they were often unappreciated and ignored when things ran smoothly. Should an accident occur on their watch, they were at best pitied, but more often ostracized and given their walking papers. Almost worse was the near miss. "Could haves" and "might haves" inflamed crews and ground-bound employees with passions that presaged the diagnostic category of "road rage." In such near misses, language could become so vile and furious that the objects of such bile could think that their omissions had launched the reign of the Antichrist.

Dwindled numbers of these "eyes of the railroad" make it hard for us to appreciate the sensitivity of their work. They were in a position to see the big picture and were thus given authority to second-guess the hurried and harried men of the surface. As Bill suggests in this account of one tower in Hopkins, Minnesota, the relationship to other rail employees was not always a warm one.

Spent some time in Tower E-14, I did. Nice enough spot on the interlocking at Hopkins. It was a busy location what with the Milwaukee main line coming through and the north-south Minneapolis & St. Louis begging for their share. We saw quite a bit of action there.

Tower operators weren't born into the job and they didn't put Joe Blow off the street up there either. Usually a tower operator started clerking, usually night clerking, which in some spots is as much about brooming as it is about railroading. But clerking is a good place to start;

you get to see how passengers and shippers feel about their time and money. You get to see the grand scheme of things and come to understand that railroads weren't put on God's Green Earth to make engineers and conductors happy.

If you work a station, a depot, or even a transfer yard shack, you see how things look from ground level. How people act when they're around trains. And they do act different! Get people around trains and they'll gawk at one while another comes right up their butt. Take the crustiest freight carman you can find, put him in Hell's central staging yard of a hundred tracks of demon freight running at ten times the yard limit, and he'll stop with his hands full of red hot tools and marvel at a shiny gondola of souls humped by the Devil's switch engine. Then he'll tell you he just stopped to look if its brake gear was in order.

Anyway, you learn things on the ground that you need to know later up in the tower. The safety stuff is the most important. You learn the lantern colors, the running lights, and the signal. You learn what the switch stands look like from different angles. You learn the sounds of things gone wrong. You learn these things on the ground and they're easier to remember up in the air. Up where the air and the mind are a bit clearer. You would be amazed how wise old yard workers can forget something down in the dust and fumes, how a veteran crew can let the clock override their brains, and how a trainmaster can let better judgment fly out the window when he wants to show he's in charge. Bring them up in the tower and it's a whole new perspective.

In the few times I hosted nonoperators up in my little nest, I was tickled by their response. It was always one of eyes widening. But ask what they saw and they fell into two distinct and opposite classes. The grease monkeys and laborers would always say it made the railroad look small to be seen from above, like a model train layout. I guess that's because on the ground they were dwarfed by the equipment. The train crews saw it different. From the tower, railroading looked bigger, almost transcontinental. For an instant they saw the panorama, not the trip segments, grades, wyes, bridges, and yard limits ticked off like notches on a gun. Then they'd stuff that notion back down their overalls because it threatened their view that they, personally, were the center of the railroad universe.

Of course they felt the same about us. Well, not the same. They were more emotional about it. For tower operators it was always a matter of one judgment call against another using instinct and the best information possible. There might be an argument or even an investigation. Then it was over. Not for crews, it was a lifelong feud, a simmering grudge carried to their graves on the wings of their high blood pressure. While other railroad employees joked about our "high altitude railroading" in the towers, the crews mocked us with the label "high attitude railroading."

Tower operators don't just learn of this problem with the crews on their first day up in the air. If they have any brains at all, they pick up on it while clerking. My first lesson came when I was filling in and sold my first passenger tickets for the Olympian's first-class section. I followed instructions and put out the green and white lantern for a passenger stop. I learned real quick that trains like that often travel in two sections, that first class is usually the lead section, and that lead enginemen believe it is beneath them to stop at an unscheduled stop.

They blew by me like to fly as a kite. I saw them laugh and wave as they went by. The passengers, especially the ladies, were madder than wet hens and promised to write railroad management. They probably did, but no one ever did anything to a crew unless they dumped a train over.

I'm not alone in this. In retirement I've come to know operators from all over the country. Calm men who took it pretty philosophically, but nevertheless always sensed the tension from the crews. Always felt a bit outside the fraternity.

But a grander bunch you'd never meet, though each year reduces our ranks. We swap stories and photos. It's amazing how those old photos show little differences in towers. We had some fairly plain ones in these parts. Usually we'd have the straight grain elevator style, wood frame construction, maybe with some do-dads in the trim. But I've seen some fancier tower architecture. Cupolas, arched leaded-glass windows, and four-gabled cantilevered blockhouses over timber-framed lower sections. Brick ones pretty as church steeples. A few stone ones like castles. Out west some built with steel beams with little houses on top like forest ranger watchtowers. Way down south some open-screened ones like gazebos. Even heard of one in a clock tower.

At E-14 I often saw dragging brake rods and hotboxes. Minneapolis & St. Louis crews would respond, though grumbling. Milwaukee crews, despite my employment by the same master, saw it in a whole different light. I'd see smoke at a journal box lid or the sparks of a bouncing brake beam and give them the appropriate signal. But they *never* stopped.

The way they looked at it, they had only a few more miles to the yard. They didn't want to stop, lose time, get bumped from a turnaround. It was ego too—they weren't going to let some pencil pusher up in a tower keep them from completing a run. But the chances they took. We could have easily ended with major derailments instead the broke knuckles and drawbars we had. So we had me giving them hand signals and them giving me obscene gestures.

Almost had a big one though. E-14 was not a good spot in heavy traffic. The background noise sometimes made it hard to hear the approach signals. Toward the end of my time I had one big freight rumbling through that was as ugly a collection of rocking boxcars and gear-dragging gondolas as you'd ever see. I didn't hear the signal ring. I still had the south end of the Minneapolis & St. Louis blocked when I saw smoke fast out of the horizon. I started to hear the screech of cast-iron brake shoes just as I pulled the clear signal. I could see them swearing as they went through.

For that one day at least, I had something in common with that crew. We shared a few moments of rapid heartbeat and adrenaline. Maybe we even shared a prayer of thanks.

CABOOSE NO. 992094

Cabooses generate affection on many levels and in many quarters. They were the center of the freight conductor's universe. But they were the eye-catchers at the end of many a train remembered from youth. They had a core of fans as loyal as the adherents of locomotives.

Identity and personality were often attributed to individual cabooses in the days before equipment pooling. In those times conductors were assigned specific cabooses, and the link between man and caboose was reinforced in the public eye. Pooling, an outgrowth of the World War II need to maximize efficiency in use of rolling stock, spelled an end to individual conductor assignments. It became theoretically possible for a caboose to travel every inch of a home railroad system of thousands of miles and sometimes serve on other adjacent lines.

Carmen continued their love affair with cabooses, especially on the Milwaukee Road. A carman would just be more likely to remember a specific caboose, remember the year he put in a new brass journal bearing or the time he welded a diamond plate on the platform deck after the caboose was "rear-ended" in the yard. On the Milwaukee Road, carmen also remembered because many had helped build or rehabilitate cabooses in the Milwaukee Shops.

Dutch has the special affection of one who spent every workday between 1946 and 1980 in the shops beneath the 35th Street bridge in Milwaukee, usually working on cabooses. But Dutch takes his relationship further than most. When Dutch speaks about cabooses from his hillside home overlooking County Stadium, he speaks as a caboose. No kidding!

I'm Caboose Number 992094, born 2094 in the Milwaukee Shops into the steel ribside family in 1951. So I'm coming up on my fiftieth birthday. Railroaders often called me a ribber, a ribsider, a conductor hut, a pumpkin shack, and, I'm embarrassed to say, an outhouse on tracks. Old Martin, my first conductor on Lines West, fondly called me "Little 94."

Ours was the seventh generation of Milwaukee Road steel ribsides and we were the last of the family to come out of the shops. The Class of '51 was the only year with fully riveted seams and joints, which made us stronger at the corners and on the bay windows. If I must say, we were the strongest in our family line, taking the rivets and the strong underframe into account.

It's true we continued the improvements made on the Class of '49. They showed the way with the drop center trucks that made for a ride like a passenger coach. And those shop boys learned a lot from the Classes of '39, '40, '41, '44, and '46 too. Hundreds of ribsiders went before us and none came after us.

We owed our existences to all the other caboose families that came out of the shops, from the first wood cupola caboose to the last steel cupola drover's caboose. Even to the terminal cabooses built on the frames of old coal tenders and the cobbled cabooses from wrecks. After that it was nothing but interlopers, a hundred cabooses from Thrall Car in 1956 and a bunch from International Car Company in 1973. But we were the last to proudly say that we were born in the Milwaukee Shops.

And I sure was proud when I rolled out in 1951. Felt lucky, too, got to ride as an extra all the way out the main line to Puget Sound in Washington State. That's were I met Old Martin the conductor.

When we first met he thumped my door and pronounced me "tight as a drum." On our first run up through the Cascades, where the grades are sharp and the curves are longest, he smiled and said, "Darn good ride." He had spent many a year in the old cupolas and was glad to have my leg room for his lanky frame.

He taught me what I know about cabooses and railroading. Not that he knew I was listening in. Old Martin was not the only conductor that thought he was just talking to himself, musing on a life spent in cabooses, engine cabs, and yard shacks. Though he couldn't hear me, like all conductors, he could sense the signals I was sending him in my sounds and vibrations.

It was kind of nice, though, when there was a real conversation in my comfy space. Nice to hear those deadheading brakemen and conductors swapping tall tales. Reassuring to listen to the carmen jawing and clanking their tools on their way to a train wreck. Funny to take in the raw language of the crusty hobos that Old Martin's sympathy and shared arthritis took as tickets in our private orange coach.

Old Martin retired in 1955 and I was put back in the transcontinental pool. Saw a lot of Idaho, Montana, South Dakota, and Minnesota. Traveled behind plenty of lumber, gravel, grain, and ore. Even took a turn as a drover's caboose on a run for cattle at the Sappington Hereford Ranch in Montana, me and two Little Joe engines and eleven livestock cars.

Then in 1958 there was the little bang-up in Terry, Montana. Coupler torn out of me out at the steel truss Calypso Bridge. Sat in Terry for a long time. When they fixed me up I had an adventure. Milwaukee's line was out and we had an emergency switchover to the Northern Pacific line north of us.

My next assignment was in Butte, Montana. The big job there had to do with Anaconda Copper Company and the mine. Lots of runs back and forth behind ore cars and steeple-cab switchers. Barely any chance to allow me to rest in the Butte yard and look at the depot clocktower and the old wooden cars waiting for salvage.

After that I got a little makeover at Deer Lodge, Montana. That was the Milwaukee Road's big spot in the Rockies for engine repair, but they could doctor cabooses there too. It was 1963 and I got the first good cleaning of my life. Rebuilt wheel trucks, too. Then back to transcontinental freight service, starting with a long slow trip up the grade we shared with Northern Pacific.

And that's how I spent most of my time on Lines West. Back and forth on long freights. Had another little incident in Nine Mile Tunnel on the Clark Fork River. They limped me around through 1970 until someone bad ordered me in Miles City, Montana. So I sat there a couple months until they decided whether to fix me or scrap me. Sat there and watched the section crews sneak their girlfriends into the old Women's Club building. Sat there and watched train crews trudge by me toward the Gordon Street boardinghouse.

Finally, some bigwig from the Mechanical Division spotted me and sent me back to Deer Lodge. A little welding, a little heat from acetylene torches, some bolts, and some plates, and I was back in business. Made my comeback run on a hospital train all the way to Milwaukee.

Back to the Milwaukee Shops twenty years after I came out of them. Well, I didn't get to go in, but I saw the old homestead and took a breather on the yard. Then it was back out on the line. Bouncing here and there around Chicago and Bensenville, then Freeport and a trip through Monroe to the old Mineral Point line where some old cars needed an escort back to some sly carmen in Milwaukee who coveted their parts.

After that I was slated to finish my days as a yard caboose in St. Paul. It was a bit beneath my dignity to replace a terminal caboose, but I concede that the years and miles had not been kind to me. Only the high mortality among the older ribsiders put me back into the pool and on my way west to Puget Sound again.

Out in the Pacific Northwest I stayed until the troubles of the Milwaukee Road bankruptcy shook the system. In the summer of 1978 I brought up the rear on another hospital train. The federal rehabilitation project rebuilt the main line and sent a lot of us cabooses into the shops for one last upgrade in 1979. That's when I got a new rolling bearing generator, spiffy platform whistles, and solid air brake pipes. When I rolled off the shops' caboose line in early 1980, I heard that there was no question about seeing Puget Sound. At least I would see Montana again.

I did. But for only two months. Then Milwaukee Road shut down in Montana for good, with lines abandoned or carved up by Burlington Northern and others. I was surplus now and sent back to Bensenville to sit on a storage track. The new ownership did not see me as worthy of further operation. So I was never blackbearded and relettered for Soo Line service.

So I sat and sat. The caboose era was over. But here and there, those who loved the ribsiders sought us out. One by one we're finding homes in places where people love trains and cherish cabooses. Hey, how about me? I'm going to Monroe, Wisconsin! A caboose could do a lot worse than a town with an old Milwaukee Road depot, good cheese, and Huber beer.

TIES THAT BIND

Almost every rail trade has an industrial counterpart. The trainmen have their fuzzy mirror image in the test crews in the big locomotive works, the freight carmen their faint reflection in the manufacturers' car shops, the machinists their fraternal bonds to lathe and mill operators of every breed. Some presume that the work of ties and rails is solely the province of rail workers, with no factory or manufacturing twin. While it would indeed be a stretch to equate the laying of rail with the forging of rail in the mills of sooty steel towns, a firmer connection does exist between the section crews and the makers of ties.

Folklore and history tell us that these brawny fellows were one and the same in the early days of laying track. In many areas around the Great Lakes, section crews felled trees in the right-of-way, cut them to gauge size, and hewed flat edges for the rail to rest on. Specialization soon followed, with the best woodsmen tackling the timber, the more deft hands hewing the wood, and the strongest backs laying the finished ties. That, too, was a passing phase, as timber grew scarcer in the areas with the most rail activity. Railroads soon had to contract for the production, or set up their own milling facilities.

Perhaps the most legendary of such tie plants was the big mill at Escanaba, Michigan. It was the biggest facility of its type owned by a railroad, in this case, the Chicago & North Western. It was the glue that held Escanaba together for over six decades. And it was the magnet that drew many colorful characters into the area.

Red Joe, an unrepentant Finnish American, sits in his daughter's kitchen in Marquette, Michigan, and recalls the ties and the times.

Escanaba was built on ties. That's right, ties, not iron, not lumber, and not anything else dug or stolen out of the U.P. None of that stuff had any significance until railroads came to haul it. And that meant ties. You might say tie makers and tie handlers were the original Yoopers, if'n you don't count Chippewas, which'n you better.

Many a man fed a family off of tie money, starting with the double-bit axe boys who homesteaded up here after the Civil War, to the machine operators during the final days of the mill. Norwegians, Swedes, Poles, Ukrainians, and, of course, Finns. There were other groups, too, from old eastern stock, to the stocky Germans. But it was those Baltic and Norse people who hung in, generation after generation, with the hard work on that stingy plot of ground. Stubborn, I guess.

There's a lot of history there and somebody ought to write the whole story. If'n there was someone know'n it. Like a good long life, it came in stages of know'n and grow'n. First, the pioneer days of dried moose meat and salt fish. Then, the boom of speculators, saloons, fancy gals, and high stakes poker. Finally, the fighting and scrapping that came as we rode the place down the old flusher of history.

Put'n the first two stages together is a job for professors and Ouija boards, and I know noth'n about either. But I do know a thing or a hundred and two about the last blast, last gasp, and the last passing of gas at our dearly departed tie mill. That's where I entered the picture. I was born in 1920, just as Escanaba was going through seizures trying to figure if'n we was headed for prosperity or the big flush. Big schemes and big dreams in those times. And Finns not too long off the boat like the Old Man were ripe for pelting. Fast talkers swindled him several times. By the time I was ten years old there was no doubt about the big flush—the family was circling the bowl. In '32, the Old Man died cutting tie poles in the woods. Something dropped on him, so he never got to hear President Roosevelt tell him about the New Deal. My uncles got me on the tie mill at age sixteen, much to the resentment of many family men grubbing on government relief.

I considered myself damn lucky to be working at first. My mother and younger brothers looked at my puny paycheck like the second coming of Jesus on the ice cream truck. Wasn't too long before I thought I'd taken up an apprenticeship with Old Pitchfork Buck down in his fiery basement. If'n you never pulled a shift in a tie mill, you'd never know what miserable work it is. It shortened a lot of lives. Not usually by killing outright. But it made a lot of strong men look forward to the day when they could take the last dump. You seldom heard them talk about retirement; they were used up.

By the time our Old Uncle with the billy goat beard and stars-and-stripes pajamas called me to throw lead at the Japanese down in the islands, I had done about every job in, around, about, and under the tie mill. Unloaded tie poles, cleaned gondolas, shoveled sawdust, worked the creosote tanks, loaded finished ties, marked ties, pounded split bands, and fed the milling line. When the war pulled me away for my tropical vacation I was just about in a position to move up and out to the ore dock, the royalty of Escanaba.

All the signs pointed to trouble in those days. Despite being a gold mine for the North Western, the hoity-toities that ran the railroad let the mill go to hell. They didn't fix anything. We were on our own as far as replacement parts, maintenance, and improvising our way through breakdowns. I can't be part of the thinking that railroads went down the commode through some conspiracy. No, I saw too many inbred idiots who couldn't operate the drawers on their oak desks and toured on executive railroad cars that cost more than all the parts we needed to function. But they could afford to send spies into the meetings of the Brotherhood of Maintenance of Way Employees.

When I came back from my trails and tales of the South Pacific, I looked at the tie mill in a whole new light. So did a lot of returning veterans. Once you've seen combat you don't suffer fools gladly. If'n you spend a year or three rooting Japs out of tunnels in volcanic rock, you don't have a lot of patience for business double-talk from a bunch of sissies in suits who don't know railroad ties from canned peas.

We made a tie that could last an average of thirty years. Down south and out west their ties were lucky to last twenty years and often only ten or fifteen. We had the capacity to make two million ties a year, if'n the tie poles could have come in fast enough. We got up to a million and a half two or three times that I know. When I was lead on the milling line, we did six thousand a day. We took care of the whole CNW system and then some. We made plenty of ties to order for contractors, the government, and other rail-roads. As far as I know, we were the only source of the 24-foot switch tie.

We emptied the U.P. of trees fit for tie poles. We're talking cull trees here, ones not of grade for finished lumber. Then we cleaned out northern Wisconsin and northern Minnesota. Finally, fifty and sixty gondola cars at a time brought up timber from Arkansas and Missouri.

That marked a change, too, I guess. Pulp became king here in the North Woods. So we weren't harvesting timber anymore up here. We were growing a crop so city folk could wipe their behinds. So the forests weren't managed for hardwoods anymore.

After the war it was all downhill. I came back to a mill that could have blown away in a summer breeze. Old farts and kids had limped it through the war, but in a way that let the equipment and buildings deteriorate shamefully. My first day back on the milling line I couldn't find a single lubricant fitting or cup that had so much as a drop of grease in it. The line trams were worn down to paper-thin steel in some places. It was a wonder that no one had been killed on that old junk pile.

It was real clear by the late forties that our days were numbered. Rumors started about shutting her down or selling her off. Then we did have some bad accidents. Some limbs lost, I recall. Next came the wildcat strikes, with punches thrown and noses bloodied.

Then came the fifties. Men were let go. All the woodcutting jobs were axed. The Escanaba car shops were closed as an omen of the end of the line. A hundred jobs trickled away. No one who left was ever replaced. Then the tie poles stopped arriving and some were even reloaded and shipped out on Illinois Central gondolas. They never had the honesty or manliness to tell us a thing.

It went out with a whimper in 1954. Sold off to a private operator who ran it into the ground even more. Some of us were offered jobs there, but why work in a scrap yard. That's how it ended up.

My North Western days finished up on the section gang. I remember the day the passenger trains ended in the late sixties. I was retired when the Union Pacific took over the last iron range track in the nineties. People talk about my connection to the CNW. Horse apples! If'n they knew anything about those days they'd know about the ties that mattered to me and still keep me think'n about Escanaba.

TENDER BOY

Few railroad stories involve youngsters as rail employees. In the seniority conscious railroad world, train tales are often the province of those snowy of hair and weathered of skin. Yet, many a rail veteran could, like early American militia drummer boys or underage seamen mustered in the time of war, recall memories from tender years in an adult job. As with those youth engaged in military service, the manpower shortages occasioned by war might account for rail officialdom's lapses in verifying applicants' ages. After demobilization, company managers and military recruiters alike would offer the same disclaimer: he looked big for his age.

When questioned about the lack of youthful accounts, my sources offered several explanations. A few underage rail employees parlayed their chronological deception into full careers and tidy pensions based on false ages. Other old-timers, products of a job world where inexperience is the gravest sin, found memories of their greenhorn years too painful for remembrance. The consensus advice offered by the wise trainmen was to look for those with a brief youthful rail encounter.

Morris fit the bill. Now retired from his own mechanical engineering firm, this former Korean War platoon leader and world traveler could tell many stories. But his favorites are from his year and a half as a boy in the roundhouses around East St. Louis, Illinois, not far from his current Mississippi River summer home.

The St. Louis Gateway, now there was a railroad. A classic train operation in as good a hub as you'd find in those times outside of Chicago. We had it all down there in those days: the crossings, the interlockings, and the traffic of a world war. It was hard as a boy to watch it from the sidelines. But I got to catch the last of it in 1945.

Had a relative sneak me in as a "tender boy," a year under age after the recruiting sergeant already turned me down. I wasn't the only one. The roundhouse I started at was full of boys under the mean eyes of railroad Methuselahs. Heck, in a rail town like ours, the competing lines would even try to steal boys away from each other. That way they could say that a youngster must be old enough if he was working for another railroad.

Tender boys had the worst of the lot for youngsters on the rails. It was dirty work and they treated us like the lowest of the low. It wasn't as brutal as section work. But if a big strapping farm boy could wrestle ties and rails with the men, well, they pretty much treated him as an equal. Heck, the section men were so happy to have some wear and tear off their aching joints, that a boy with big hands and a muscular back could expect to get treated to shots and beers, and maybe even Friday night in a cathouse.

Not so with tender boys. Word of the end of serfdom had not reached the ears of those ancient engine oilers who ran those roadhouses like POW camp commandants. Put aside those stories you've heard about sadistic nuns in parochial schools, basic training drill instructors, and fiendish camp counselors. An aged roundhouse man, his bones wracked by arthritis, his brain addled by fumes, and his heart as black as the cinders in the ash pit, well, no meaner creature existed in 1945 America.

Tender boys were put on Earth only to provide outlets for the loathing felt by roundhouse workers for their fellow man. Our sufferings were grist for their humor. Our injuries were affronts to their tight schedules. We were beneath contempt and could be shown no quarter in the battle against the clock and no mercy during the alternate sweltering and freezing that dominated the roundhouse calendar.

Tender boys were so named due to the one key duty they were allotted in the highly stratified pecking order of a large roundhouse. Our main assignment was to grease fittings on the locomotive tenders. That job we had to do without fail, despite the combined efforts of everyone in the roundhouse to make sure that the task was made as unsafe and nigh unto impossible as possible. And, if circumstances allowed us breath enough and continuing attachment of all limbs and digits, we were encouraged to oil the dynamo reservoirs and wipe off the headlamp. If any time remained beyond those tasks we were fair game for any personal service required by oilers, hostlers, boilermen, or machinists. This could include anything from an errand to retrieving a plug of chewing tobacco from a hostler's car or the ever popular command to fetch mythical tools, such as the left-handed spud wrench or the upside-down hammer.

Hostlers were our main protagonists. They were always in a hurry, always trying to set new records for quick service turnaround, even if the engine wasn't needed for hours. This hurrying meant that watching out for tender boys was not their highest priority. Never mind if we were still under the tender when they decided an engine was going out the door.

This was wartime, of course. No time for idle engine sitting on service tracks. Even the Gateway had the bustle that came with moving military supplies, weapons, and troops. And we were still one hundred percent steam in 1945. At least in our roundhouse. Seems like a curiosity of an Alco diesel came through, but I could have that confused with something I saw across the river in the Minneapolis & St. Louis yard.

It was a hostler in a hurry who almost killed me on my second week on the job. I had the job down pretty quick, what with family coaching and all. It wasn't exactly brain surgery after all and I was pretty nimble. But not nimble enough for this one old fellow brought out of his likely asylum confinement to torture tender boys. Every thirty seconds it was "move your blankety-blank butt" out of his mouth. Well, actually, it was urging of a far more indelicate variety, but you get the drift.

I think this fellow had it out for me. Something to do with a relative of mine getting a job the hostler had pegged as his own. He got a big kick out of starting to move before all my gear was out of the way. But this one time he didn't even see me. Not that every hostler didn't recognize the look of our blue carts.

Each tender boy had a cart with a grease pump, oil cans, wiping rags, and simple tools. That was the thing in the roundhouse, every group had its own distinctive paraphernalia, a cart or toolbox. That went for firebox attendants, ash cleaners, electricians, inspectors, and so forth.

In that time we were given only fifteen minutes per engine. We had to work fast. We had to stay out of each other's way. Or I should say, the tender boys were expected to stay out of everyone's way. And we had to look out for ourselves in all this jostling.

Everybody knows how dangerous it is in a railyard, on a rip track, or in a car shop. But few understand the hazards of a big roundhouse in a busy time. Not just from crazy hostlers, but from leaking hot water, bursts of steam, dropped tools and parts from men working up on the engine, the infernal ash pit, and being caught underneath when the engine moved.

When they trained you, they warned you about all these things and quite a few others. But they so scared the bejeebers out of us about the ash pit that it probably caused other accidents. Everybody seemed to keep one eye on the ash pit, looking over their shoulders at the ash pit, and wondering who was closest to the ash pit at any given moment. The thing about the ash pit, you see, was that it had a deceptive cinder crust over a pool of hot slurry and water. Hot enough to cook you if you fell through!

So we lived in fear that we'd fall through or in morbid fascination that someone else would. It made you unmindful of almost everything else. Even of murderous hostlers.

But on my fateful day my mind wasn't just on the ash pit. Early in the day I spotted a greasy silver dollar on the service track. I aimed to make it mine as soon as I could. But the way we were watched I couldn't just bend over when it was in the clear between engines. No, I had to hatch a plan. I thought if I could get a tender parked right over it, then I could scamper under the tender and pluck it up. So I contrived to spot the engine and tender a little off spot of their usual marks. Nudge the machinist's toolbox onto the tracks here, get my blue cart in the way there, and clumsily knock over the cleaning barrel somewhere else. I thought I was real cute and real smart.

Finally, the ducks all fell in line and an engine and a tender were right in position. All I had to do was dip under the tender sill. Then there I was, the silver dollar in reach. What should happen, but the roundhouse foreman yelled on our service track to reposition for heavier maintenance. That meant a switch to the opposite side. So the hostler gave the signal and pulled away. Right over me!

Now as impressive as a steam engine is from the side, the big old locomotives are very humbling if they're passing over the top of you. You can see all sorts of things that you normally wouldn't see. The dark underbelly as it were. And a goodly dosage of the aforementioned steam and water, plus some hot grease and oil dripping down your face.

But as great as my fear was as it passed over me, my embarrassment outstripped it when I was exposed to the world after the engine and tender pulled away. I soon became an object of amazement, gawking, and ridicule. But the final chapter was yet to come. My hostler nemesis approached me with a sadistic smile and jaunty gait.

"I was going to ask for my dollar back," he smirked, "but I figure you earned it today."

TOWER TIMES

Railroad work has changed over the years with the advent of new technology, the rise of the short lines, and the continual drive to cut labor costs. Like many other sectors of the American economy, jobs that once seemed indispensable are now blown away like autumn leaves before the November winds. Among these casualties, railroad tower operators were once thought to be the most secure.

Tower operators ascended to prominence in the golden age of railroading. The spreading network of tracks and crossings, and multiple trains on the same lines, created the need for greater vigilance. Collisions, often spectacular and fatal, proved that the old system founded on low density traffic could not cope with more speed, longer trains, and critically timed train movements.

Part fire tower watchman, part air traffic controller, and part dispatching clerk, the railroad tower operator presaged the complexities of modern transportation movement. In their day, these operators brought human eyes, ears, and mental acuity to tasks now performed by electronic circuity, sensors, and computer chips. Almost every section of the crisscrossed Midwest has a story of a potentially horrible train wreck narrowly averted by timely tower operator action.

Yet because they were out of view of the public and not hands-on with the rolling stock, tower operators were seldom romanticized or even respected. Train crews often ridiculed the tower operators and tried to deflect blame onto them. Tower operators made judgment calls, and their judgment was routinely questioned by management and other workers. The phrases "darned if you do, darned if you don't," "no-win situation," and "lose-lose proposition" were probably first uttered in a railroad tower.

This does not mean that former tower operators with fond memories cannot be found. Many are lifelong rail fans who went on to successful careers in other trades and professions. William of St. Cloud, Minnesota, is among those proud ranks. He is perched in a turret of his Victorian era home and primed for a tower story.

Tower E-122 was my home during the last two years of World War II. Just a young fellow on the Milwaukee Road in the busiest time in railroad history. The tower was two miles west of Granite Falls, Minnesota, smack on the crossing of the Milwaukee Road and the Great Northern. It wasn't the busiest spot on either line, but it sure kept me busy in the learning stages of my employment. Probably wasn't the best assignment for a greenhorn.

The war years were noted for short training phases. They pushed us out of the nest real quick. The older fellows were kind of worn out by '44. Most would have retired if not for the labor shortages. Many treated the war as a personal inconvenience. But for us younger guys who couldn't get into military service, the war was our opportunity to get a rail job and contribute to the war effort.

They didn't really tell us that the days of the towers were numbered or that electronic signals were already on the drawing boards. They never told me that I would end up clerking in a depot after my stint in the tower. No, all they told me during my orientation was that a tower operator was the king of railroad safety. They told us that and two contradictory instructions. First, safety was the most important duty. Second, that war matériel freight must be expedited in every way possible. They gave us no clue as to how to reconcile those directives.

It was a good job for a young man, especially if you weren't afraid of some responsibility. And if you didn't have a thin skin. There was always somebody yelling at me. But I grew up around several hard-of-hearing family members, so I never took yelling personally. It was the cussing I didn't care for. Not that I'm a prude. And railroaders in general can go toe to toe with the saltiest one-eyed tattooed sailors when it comes to blue language. But when the profanities are directed at you personally and cuttingly, well, then it's going to get to you no matter how much you pretend it isn't.

That kind of obscene and targeted swearing, the kind maligning God, your mother, and the founding fathers, wasn't a general response. A yard-master might swear in exasperation. A roving railroad executive might step off his private car and swear just to prove he could do it. By the way, I remember one high level company man who dabbed the corners of his mouth with a silk handkerchief as if cuss words were gravy dribbling down his weak chin. A fellow operator, a yard freight clerk, or a station agent might swear as a sign of kinship. The carmen, roundhouse workers, section crews, and tradesmen swore just to emphasize that they were dirt encrusted and calloused, whereas we were pale and broad of butt. It was the train crews who reached deep into the quiver of their poison arrows and dug out the most lethal and profane projectiles to launch into the hides of tower operators.

Let's face it, most train crews thought that they were the railroad and the rest of us were superfluous. Like all large enterprises, railroads are sprawling and bumbling empires teeming with thousands of botched details. Train crews saw themselves as above this chaos and viewed the rest of us with the contempt usually reserved for criminally inclined mental defectives. So, yes, they did cuss at us in the most pointed and vile ways imaginable.

They cussed us for good reasons, bad reasons, and no reasons at all. They cussed until their faces were crimson, their neck veins on the verge of explosion, and their arms weary from shaking fists in our faces. They aligned cuss words in continuously new and imaginative sequences that communicated both their creativity and their bile. They cussed until they were totally spent, like the great beasts in spring combat. And yet they always concluded with a look of regret. Not for our gentle souls or for their own breach of the peace. No, it was regret for the inadequacy of human language. These trainmen left unsatisfied because they lacked terms sufficiently hateful, dismissive, and ridiculing to the office of tower operator.

Their cussing had a pecking order not unlike their status arrangements on the train. A respected passenger run, not a local, was on top. After the passenger crews came the scheduled main line freights, then the way freights, and the yard switching crews. The higher the rank, the more pronounced the cussing.

With the crews, the normal pecking order was honored. The conductors usually led the warrior party circling the doomed like vultures. The brakemen made quick stabbing probes. The engineers were like fat old chieftains who waddled in at the honor of thrusting the final and fatal spear into the already crippled victim. The firemen simply aped their leaders with epithets that echoed the engineers like hissing steam.

Now, you might ask, how did a tower operator get to understand railroad sociology from up in a high altitude nest? Well, you can see a lot from up there. If you're near a yard, you can watch drama unfold. If you're at a crossing out in the middle of nowhere, there are quirks to observe, train crews that get out to stretch and complain, maintenance men who stop to eat their lunches, and managers who try to catch you napping.

Not that there isn't plenty of solitary time. Sometimes hours of silence. Sometimes days with nothing more than short commands. But that left plenty of time to think. Time to think about the railroad scheme of things. It might have been better for the railroads if the other employees had done some thinking, instead of huffing, puffing, and cussing their way toward retirement.

Even with the isolation, there were also stressful times in the towers. I sure had some moments at Tower E-122. Anytime you have interlockings and crossings between different railroad systems it made for some tough moments. Especially since it involved the Great Northern. The Milwaukee Road crews had little use for us. But the GN boys saw us as heathen vermin. I came into that tower at age eighteen and was a target for those goat thumpers from day one. They never missed a chance to belittle me and question my competency.

It came to a head one balmy summer night. I was working third trick, the midnight to 8 A.M. shift. I had two eastbound freights hauling military matériel coming toward me out of Montevideo. They were about ten miles off. I also had a late northbound goat wagon, which is what we called GN passenger trains, about eight miles out.

Now, the problem was that the goat wagon needed to make a Willmar connection and was already running tight. So what do I do? I had three trains in my signal area and a number of unanswered questions. The goat wagon didn't seem like it was running its normal speed. On the other hand, the freights were on the approach of a four-mile grade and I could stall them out if I slowed them. Then there was the question of the size of the interval between the freights.

If I let the goat wagon run I might get a situation where the lead freight might hit it. Was there a big enough hole to fit the passenger train in between the two freights? With modern technology these are easy questions, but in those days all you had was instinct and information one step above the Ouija board and astrology.

I had to make a decision, so I stopped the Great Northern passenger train. It seemed to me I was serving two priorities: safety and expediting war matériel. And I was violating only one priority: passenger scheduling. The mathematics were clear to me, two rights outweighed one wrong.

The stopped GN crew didn't see it my way. The conductor strutted up to the base of the tower, kicked the cinders and ballast like a baseball manager might at the adverse call of an umpire, looked up at me with vicious eyes, and started to scream.

"Idiot. Moron. Retarded hayseed. Inbred son of a sow. Is this your first day on the job? Did you ever see a passenger train before they took you away from slopping hogs? Did the fumes from all that chicken coop shoveling addle your brain? Couldn't your father keep you mother from breeding with the livestock? How about you and your sister up there put your pants back on and watch what's going on down here on the tracks? That is, if you can fish your glasses out of your underpants."

He got real mean and the genuine cussing began. He threatened to probe various parts of my body with every railroad tool made. He promised a collection of tortures more complete than the practices later testified to at the Nuremberg war crimes trials. He was especially gleeful about removal of my head so he could put it to use as a toilet, bowling ball, fish-gutting board, urinal, probe of cattle intestinal tracts, and septic tank cleaning brush. Of course he was a bit more colorful about it.

Then, as if heaven sent reprieve, the first freight thundered through. I don't know if his tirade stopped immediately or if the freight drowned him out. His face was in a shadow. I did see his face as he turned his head to note the flats of army trucks and artillery pieces. I could see that the war matériel scored points on my behalf. I kept silent about my suspicion that substantial amounts of war matériel were circulating on America's vast rail network without ever reaching our troops. At least I was sure that one distinctive weapons consignment passed Tower E-122 at least three times in 1944. But why should I trouble the conductor with supply problems and shifts in military strategy?

I shouted down to him triumphantly, "The second one is close behind." I drummed my finger jubilantly on the operators table and hummed "When Johnny Comes Marching Home," making my "hurrahs" as close to the steam train sound as possible. I ran through that several times and then switched over to "Washington Post March."

My celebration started to wither as the sound of the first freight faded into silence. The approach sounds of the second should have already been audible. I waited five minutes, ten minutes, fifteen minutes. Back to the tower hustle the conductor and brakeman. Their cussing could be heard a good hundred yards distant.

This time the brakeman acted as spokesperson and inquisitor. He yelled, cajoled, threatened, whined, and sputtered. He accused me of drunkenness, imbecility, excessive self-pleasuring, and left-wing politics. Finally, he drew up his considerable gut and puffed out his chest in a posture worthy of an infuriated Moses before an irrational Pharaoh.

"Let our train go!" he thundered.

Their harangue took on an added feature when an old Swedish lady joined them. This elderly passenger leaned on a cane but had spring in her step. Even in the dim light it was clear that she was perturbed at the delay. The conductor and brakeman were probably more shocked than I when the old lady commenced cussing at a rather manly level. She was impressive in her broken English and I assume her best efforts were contained in her lapses into Swedish. Soon she was joined by other passengers and a babel of profane Swedish convected up my way on the hot air of hatred.

I felt a little bit like Doctor Frankenstein in the movie scene where the townspeople storm the castle. It would not have surprised me if they had rocked the tower off its foundations.

The mob was debating what to do with me when the second freight rumbled through. It contained no redeeming war matériel, instead being a consist of empty cattle cars. Naturally, the folks were none too pleased to see the cause of their delay. I did offer the lame and spontaneous excuse that the cars were needed to haul beef to a cannery under contract to the military.

A final shake of the fist from the brakeman and a promise of reporting the incident from the conductor were the closing scene of this one-act play. The conductor made his report and I was interviewed by investigators from the Milwaukee Road, Great Northern, and the federal government. My bosses quaked in their boots and train crews happily looked forward to my discharge. But I was cleared on all counts. Wartime thinking saved my butt.

Now when people asked me what I did in World War II, I tell them I did my time in the tower. They don't know what to make of that. Some think that I must have been a guard, a prisoner, a sentry, or an observer at an airfield. Nowadays who would understand tower time?

OKTOBERFEST SPECIAL

Passenger train fans have many fond memories of "special" trains. Specials were often excursion trains running to athletic events, conventions, and seasonal tourist attractions. The term had broader application, including unscheduled freight and work trains on some railroads.

The general public was usually unaware that railroad employees also used the term special *in a humorous way. For them the whispered mention of a special told of an unauthorized use of a train, usually the engine. It was a rare but not unheard of form of joyriding. The offense could prompt discharge if management heard of an incident and could prove it. Usually the proof element was lacking, as yard workers claimed preoccupation with other tasks.*

La Crosse's reputation as a rail town alone makes it a likely site for exuberant rail tales. Add the usually friendly and sometimes rowdy rivalry between the partisans of the Milwaukee Road and those of the Burlington Northern, and you have a tradition of one-upmanship. Cap off that with the western Wisconsin city's credentials for letting the good times roll and an environment in which any story, no matter how outrageous, could be based in fact.

Tavern life in this river town is on a high order, with a lively downtown and many vibrant neighborhood bars and outlying beer joints. Festivals and entertainment abound, especially in the warm months. Of these events, the annual Oktoberfest holds the deepest cultural niche in the area's northern European population and the warmest spot in the hearts of blue-collar beer drinkers.

La Crosse's Oktoberfest has generated thousands of stories, with more than a few having a rail connection. They include the lessons in excess learned by one out-of-town trainman in the 1970s who recounted a lost weekend that ends with his waking up handcuffed to a parking meter and with a nuclear headache on Sunday, with no intervening memory since Friday afternoon. They also number items on the folklore of fatigue, such as a Milwaukee Road crew who all dozed off, failed to stop, and ran right through the La Crosse yard.

Danny, former carman and roundhouse worker on the Milwaukee Road, knows that beer is not the only element of Oktoberfest that causes mental lapses. Now securely married and the father of teenagers, he remembers a time of silliness undertaken in the days of sowing wild oats. He pays for a round of beer at the Oktoberfest pavilion and drifts back to a summer more than twenty years ago.

You guys remember what it was like back then, don't you. We all thought we were John Travolta in *Saturday Night Fever.* Well, maybe some lower rent version of that. Anyway, the feeling was the spirit of anything goes. We had a lot of younger fellows on the railroad at that time, coming in to replace the last of those steam era guys. So the railroads were still getting used to long hair and beards.

Oktoberfest was a big event for the young railworkers. Naturally, the largest contingents were from Milwaukee Road and BN. But we always ran into our counterparts from Soo Line, North Western, and Green Bay and Western. Even some from Rock Island and Illinois Central would drift in.

Now, you realize that we weren't coming to Oktoberfest to meet railworkers. No, it was for the young ladies. Gals who liked railroaders and beer. Don't get me wrong, even in those looser times, railroaders didn't draw the girls like pro athletes or doctors. But Oktoberfest did pull in the ones who liked us.

And could they drink beer. We've all known one-drink women and cleaned up their second drink out of our cars or off our shoes. But Oktoberfest always drew heartier gals looking to party with railers or brewery workers. Lots of local women, but many from all over western Wisconsin, Iowa, and Minnesota. Lot of farm gals.

As my better half says, only a farm girl would see a railroad worker as a step up. She should know, she's off the farm and married to me. My wife claims that the whole attraction of a railworker as husband is that you know he'll be gone a lot and not under foot as much as some men. But I think the steady money and benefits had something to do with it. My wife and I know one Onalaska woman who claims she married her BN hubby only so she could get her allergy shots.

I give them their due. Railroad girlfriends and rail wives are pretty good partners. They keep the home fires burning, the bills paid, and learn to unplug toilets and fix faucets real quick. They manage the checkbooks with skill and are tighter than baby shoes with a dollar. Many a railworkers' cottage or boat was paid for with money the wife set aside. And who's ever heard of the married railworker who ran out of beer money before payday? Those women really know how to budget that beer allowance.

That's why so many rail families own small businesses. Those women know how to save and invest. It's kind of a joke about all the railroad girlfriends and wives who end up running taverns and supper clubs. The main part of the joke is how the bar business works only if the man stays out of the coolers and out of the till. The real trick is to bring in the rail crowd and not give away too many drinks or let the section crews run tabs.

Anyhow, me and my carmen buddies were over from Green Bay, Wausau, and Portage to meet some Oktoberfest women. You might say we were interviewing potential railroad girlfriends. And I guess you could say they were interviewing us. What can I say? It was the seventies and there was a lot of interviewing going on.

But we no sooner showed up than we tied into some real live wires. All Minnesota gals from over in La Crescent. They seemed just barely old enough to be in the beer hall. Kind of blended hippy farm gals with a mixture of tie-dyed scarves, flannel shirts, peace sign jewelry, and jeans that had seen real work. That made them better prospects than the disco girls wandering over from the college campus. It was a good sign that they latched onto our gang, even though we were all eight to ten years older. Shows some practical thinking, having an eye that detects a man with a steady paycheck. They were just all-around versatile. They could rock to oldies and country music and they could polka. Plus they could squirm through the crowd to get beer.

We kind of paired off real quick. If we were honest about it, they did the picking, not us. That's often how it works at Oktoberfest, or how it did in my day. You might ask ten gals simply to dance and get shot down each time, and then one would just drag you off for the weekend. Sure brought out the cave woman side in some of them.

So we were getting to know each other and getting real friendly. Then they heard we worked for the railroad. Oh, they liked that. They all had something nice to say about the trains. Most had ridden the Hiawatha as little kids, even a few the Empire Builder. They started dropping hints early in the evening about how they would like a train ride.

After a couple hours of beer, conversation, and squeezes, the train ride talk grew a little more bold. They started to challenge us, suggesting that maybe we weren't really railroad workers. No matter that we confessed our carmen status and swore that deep dark secret oaths of the railroad brotherhoods forbade us from laying a hand on a locomotive. One La Crescent girl sniffed that she once had a boyfriend on a race car pit crew and that he gave her a one-lap ride in the modified stock car he worked on.

We saw that our goose was about to be cooked. Me and my buddies clearly understood that we would not progress to the next stage of our interviews until we made a concession in the train ride area. We made an offer to talk to a yard crew to see what we could do. The girls saw that as a feeble effort and suggested they just might talk to the yard crew themselves. So we were at the make-it-or-break-it phase.

Us guys did a quick huddle. We all knew the La Crosse yard. We all knew that as least one engine would be idling over there. And one guy had worked the Wausau roundhouse, so we had an operator. So we whispered plans. Shows what three hours of Old Style and Special Export will do to a man's brain. That and a serious desire for interviewing on the mind.

So a few more beers and we were all off to the yard in the pickup truck of the sole soda drinking girl in this entourage. When we got there it was all giggling and stumbling in the dark. Still, we found a yard engine idling and all climbed aboard. Two couples crammed into the cab. The rest of us took in the fresh air on the diamond plate platform and hung on to the handrail. Soon we were moving.

I really don't remember who threw which switches or how we got out on the main line. Next thing I remember we were out on a bridge over the river. We're lucky no one fell off and drowned. So we stopped on the bridge and argued about going around or back. The girls were satisfied so that settled it. Our operator backed it up all the way to the yard.

When we got there we were greeted by two La Crosse police officers and one angry yard clerk. The girls thought the lights on the police cars made it a festive occasion so they started singing, "I've Been Working on the Railroad." When the cops asked what they should do with us, the yard clerk went into the depot to make a call. I guess he was on the phone with a supervisor, and we could overhear that it was a heated conversation.

The cops gave us shrugs and looked at their watches. The older of the two told us how busy Oktoberfest was in their line of work. Finally, after waiting about ten minutes, they grew impatient with the clerk. "Don't do that again," the older cop warned, "or if you do, don't stop until you're over in Minnesota." With that admonishment, they got in their cars and left.

We slipped away and counted ourselves lucky that no one had pegged us as Milwaukee Road employees. We all would have lost our jobs in an eye blink. When I transferred over to the La Crosse car department, that clerk would look at me funny, but never placed me as part of the engine-napping crew.

I left the railroad when the Soo took over. Worked my way into management with a good company. Have a nice house and a nice family. Wife lets me run a model railroad layout in the basement. I married one of the girls from that night and never regretted it. Sometimes all we have to do is share a beer and she'll smile and say the words "Oktoberfest Special" and make a tooting sound like an engine horn.

She's still interviewing me, you know.

ACCIDENTAL CARMAN

It is difficult to determine whether more romance about railroading is derived from the long careers of crusty train crew veterans or the short sojourns of young manhood on track gangs. Both sides of the argument have many partisans, and good points are made by both on behalf of indelible imprints left on railroad souls. It is a dispute that is beyond proof or resolution.

What is known is the very real and quirky diversity of ways that railroaders came into their jobs. In the early annals of Midwest railroading, many a laborer came to the massive track projects courtesy of fugitive flight from the East or fraud and swindles of immigration agents. Later on, the "job referral" system was often through membership in fraternal orders or secret societies. Then came times of massive waves of itinerant workers, displaced sharecroppers, and strikebreakers.

Finally, hiring settled into a comfortable, if not equitable, tradition of family referrals broken only by periods of greater manpower needs.

The individual stories of hiring, initiation into work life, and ultimately settling into a rail craft are as varied as the millions who toiled in the service of railroads. Even third and fourth generation railroaders were not immune from the bewilderment that goes with a new job. But a handful of railworkers faced real shock and surprise and the nagging question: "What did I get myself into?"

Milwaukee Road veterans came to call our informant Young Dutch to differentiate him from Old Dutch in the Milwaukee Shops. Otherwise, the two needed no differentiation. They were distinct in every way except that they both were freight carmen on the Milwaukee Road during the late 1970s and early 1980s. Young Dutch takes a break from his hearing schedule and joins us for a burger and beer in a Madison, Wisconsin, tavern.

It all started when I worked for Job Service in the old Department of Industry, Labor, and Human Relations. I was hired to be the disabled veterans outreach worker in the Portage office. That was only seven years after Vietnam for me and while I was pretty much intact physically, limp and blown-out eardrum notwithstanding, I was still raw in the psyche.

College and the graduate degree were out of the way and I was really waiting to move up on the civil service list for a hearing examiner position with the state. So there I was, cooling my heels in Portage, placing vets in jobs as plastic molders and cannery line inspectors. Getting loaded with them on Friday and Saturday nights and placing them with a new employer when they missed work Mondays. Occasionally I'd get to refer one of them to a good job. A couple at the electric power plant and some on section crews on the railroad.

That was an object lesson in how the pay is better in select blue-collar occupations than in the dregs of the white-collar sector. My mind proofed out the rough calculus and told me something was amiss. We all would like money and status. But most of us will take money every time over the illusion of status and no money. So I resolved to refer myself to one of these better jobs. This meant I had to construct an appropriate job history for myself within the Job Service data base. Check a box here, fill in a blank there, and soon I was a blue-collar renaissance man—at least on paper.

So I was ready when the fellow from the Milwaukee Road walked in with the position description for the car department at the Portage yard. Freight carmen mechanic, mechanical skills required, knowledge of arc welding and acetylene cutting desirable, familiarity with pipe cutting, threading, and bending a plus. The pay was almost twice that of Job Service. I was on my way!

The Milwaukee Road wanted five referrals for two positions. So I put myself in along with one other qualified guy and loaded the rest of the list with applicants calculated to scare the bejeebers out of any sober and sane employer. When I was called for the interview, I showed up in flannel and denim and the fellow said I looked familiar. I was hired Thursday and told to start on Monday. That gave me the weekend to get to the library and read about train parts and other basic mechanical information.

Monday, me and the other new guy were put to the test right away. We were taken to a siding and told to cut up a boxcar. Two torches, some pry bars, and a couple of big hammers and the foreman leaves us with no other instructions. Well, I managed to get my torch lit with the striker but couldn't get the right gas mix, so I was cutting so slow you could have hacksawed quicker. Turns out the tank regulator was bad. My new coworker, Jerry, figured that out and we made a raid in the roundhouse and swiped their tank regulator. Then we were back in business.

It really was a test of us, not only to see if we could improvise with equipment, but also to test whether we could figure out how to cut up a car without killing each other. You learn real quick that when you cut one part away another massive piece of steel falls down. We inadvertently honed our fire-fighting skills after we set fire to the boxcar's wooden deck, which in turn set fire to dry grass and brush near the roundhouse. Good thing roundhouses have fire-fighting hoses. We also learned that when you cut heavily painted metal you get plenty of molten splatter. But at day's end the car was cut up in loading size chunks and we survived the quarter-sized splatter burns, our burnt overalls, our singed hair, and our fume-filled lungs.

So we passed the first test. But we were given many more. Jerry and I helped each other over each new hurdle with constant ribbing about the sailor helping the airman and vice versa. It wasn't the foreman who put us through the car department obstacle course. He was a decent fellow named Al, younger than us. It was two old retrobate carmen, a Mutt and Jeff odd couple out of La Crosse. A Bohemian and an Irishman, going by the names of Auchie and Babe. No one who ever worked with them on the Milwaukee Road would ever forget them.

They were dedicated to the proposition that each new carman should be made to suffer every indignity that they had endured. Never mind that they wanted us to suffer thirty years' worth during the first year on the job. Never mind that they still hated the old farts that long ago made their lives miserable. Part of the test was to see if they could run us off with dirty work and stupid errands. Oddly enough, once we passed the test they were always telling us to slow down and take it easy. Over time they changed their posture from murderous threats to our well-being to congenial annoyances. Auchie spoke a strange dialect of Casey Stengel-ese that no one could made head or tail of. Babe was continuously irritable in a way that made us laugh.

The Portage car department had one other carman when I joined it, Tony, a thirty-five-year veteran who started as a car cleaner on steam passenger trains on the Chicago & North Western. He was a real gentleman and patient with new employees. He was an excellent teacher and saved Jerry and me from many a mishap. He probably blunted many of Auchie's and Babe's planned torments of the new guys.

Tony was the mentor every new worker should have. He had me feeling like the rip track was a second home. Showed me the ropes on using the boom to move wheels, how to jack up cars, how to repack a bearing and replace air brake blocks—the whole deal from one end of a freight car to the other. As I discovered when I worked in Milwaukee, a summer with Tony was worth about two years of training elsewhere.

It wasn't long before foreman Al trusted us to work alone. Sometimes it seemed like he'd rather send the new guys out troubleshooting than Auchie and Babe. So we rehung our share of boxcar doors at area canneries, unjammed covered hoppers at the grain co-ops, patched holes on the ballast cars out on the work trains, and changed brake shoes by the hundreds on the coal cars at the Columbia power plant. Al even sent us along on a train of damaged cars headed down to Milwaukee for major repairs.

Those were busy times in Portage. There was major work going on out on the main line, heavy coal train traffic, and plenty of maintenance of way work trains. All the traffic and the rushing seemed to increase the incidence of derailments. We worked some big wrecks. Some on the main line and some out on the old tracks going eastward through the marsh country to ballast quarries.

It was hard work, but it was rewarding work. It grew on me. When the layoff at Portage came it threw me for a loop. Railroading had gotten in my blood, so I applied for a transfer to Milwaukee. Big mistake! The chaos and claustrophobia of the Milwaukee Shops did not suit me. That's when I knew it was time to get back on my professional track.

It was just a short time in my life, but it gave me a connection to railroading that hasn't left me. Twenty years later I still stop by the yards and try to find carmen. I always tell them that once upon a time I was a carman and for an accidental carman I wasn't half bad.

WORKING SECTION

It is difficult to provide a definitive look at track work. It has been different things in different times, spanning the chasm between the massive undertaking of fresh railbeds and tracks across thousands of miles of unbroken terrain and the ten minutes of clearing ice from a balky switch on a winter's morning. The unifying factor, in all times and in all places, has been the backbreaking nature of the work.

Millions of Americans have worked track construction or repair. Hardly an ethnic group in North America has missed a turn. The famous and infamous, rich and poor, city dweller and country yeoman have all had turns with hammer, pick, and bar.

For many it was a temporary job, first step up the ladder. For others it was a lark, part of a youthful adventure of hitchhiking or riding the rails. Others sought refuge from abject poverty in the rough work and were claimed in limb or life before they really learned the job. Years of railroad conversation have confirmed the notion of a broad democratic fraternity of track workers, proven through the private admission of judges, military officers, doctors, and college professors, that they too once worked as gandy dancers or section men.

Willy, an Illinois Central section crewman, had a different slice of the experience. His was not a college vacation sojourn on the rails. His was a life's work of blistered hands and exposure to the elements. At times it was a battle just to stay alive.

He reminisces from a recliner chair in a Marengo, Illinois, nursing home.

Hell's bells, nearly everybody took a turn on section work when I was a youngster. Most did a summer and were never seen again. It wasn't the sort of job that drew men who worried about chapped hands or scuffing their boots. It was the most honest and direct work that God ever set down on a man's plate.

I put in my time the real old-fashioned way. Thirty-two years on the section crew. Not many went longer than that. Not many lasted nearly that long. Couple of smashed fingers and broken toes were usually enough to scare off the fainthearted. For some, it was just a distaste for sweat rolling down their backs.

From the first ties, rails, and spikes put down, I don't think a single maintenance of way worker ever felt secure about living through a work-day. Between the heavy railroad cars, the swinging tools, the bridges, and the rough characters, it was not a place for the timid. You had to be a bit of a risk taker and yet know when to hold back from something that didn't feel right.

That was ninety percent of staying alive working section. Instinct, pure instinct. The type of thing you felt in your bones but didn't mention to another soul. You could see it in an experienced section crew. They might hold back from work on a flood-soaked levee, might be a bit slow to get out on that cracked timber bridge, or give a wide berth to the carmen pulling a car out of muck with a steel cable. Nine times out of ten, they would just miss the collapse of dirt, the crumbling of the bridge, or the snapping of the cable. The ones who didn't hold back didn't last.

That happened to me in '55. We were working on an Illinois Central bridge near Kankakee. There had been a derailment there, but without much visible damage to the bridge. As usual, the bosses wanted traffic going as soon as the tracks were cleared, never mind checking the soundness of the bridge. First train went through and we felt an out-of-place vibration. The foreman just looked at us and we all ran off that bridge. A piece of deck dropped right where we had been standing.

Another time we was working along the main line, on a switchout siding or waiting track, I believe. Trains, freights and passengers, were coming through pretty steady. Business as usual. After a while you don't really notice the trains 'cause you gotta pay attention to the work. The sound settles into your brain. Clickety-click, clickety-click. You hear it all day long. But that day on the main line a long freight was going by and there was a sudden change. It went from clickety-click to clackety-crack real quick. Twenty men ran and two didn't; they ended up in the hospital. A hopper car with a flat spot on a wheel was knocking off hunks of rail and throwing debris.

Further downstate on the main line we had a foreman who prevented a derailment just by the sound of the ring of hammer on steel. It was a real hot day and rail was expanded. He said it meant the joints between rail sections were compressed. Sure enough, he walked a bit ahead of where we were working and found a joint under so much pressure that it was buckling and the closest tie plates were working loose. The City of New Orleans had to stop, but when the train crew heard what we had found they was plenty grateful. Porters brought us ice cream and pop. Even the engineer said a nice word. Usually got as much credit as the slaves who built the pyramids.

Mostly the work was replacing ties, tightening joint bolts, jacking track to pack ballast, and placing new rails. Sometimes we would join up with other crews to rebuild whole sections of track. Sometimes we'd piss away a whole day fighting stuck doors on gravel cars. Other days we'd be slowed by loads of ties wedged too tightly in gondolas and glued together by creosote cooking out of them on a boiling hot day. It's hard to say whether the worst of it was the work or the weather.

You gotta accept the work, whatever it throws at you. It's one of the hardest jobs on Earth and you can only do it over the long haul if you decide that it won't whip you. But some of it gets to you. For me it was bridges and the big yards. Bridges, hell, you're always dropping tools. Worse is falling off slippery decks. Worst still, slipping through the deck and catching a tie or rail in the balls. The big yards were just too much commotion, especially where you had main lines right through the yard.

Switch engines banging cars, idling big locomotives, and trains passing. Too damn easy to get distracted and turn around right in the path of a highballing express.

The weather! Don't get me started! You work section on the IC and you get it coming and going. In my time I saw section men drop of heat stroke, lose fingers and toes to frostbite, get hit by lightning, get swept away by an ice jam, and get buried under ties dumped by twisters. Bless that Midwest weather—a little bit of Canada and a little bit of Texas.

But it wasn't all bad stuff. We had ball games at lunch on those two or three days of spring and fall that we get in those parts. We had washtubs of ice cold beer after work. Then there were rides in handcars and motorcars on the tracks squeezing in between the freights. Plus on the IC we occasionally had that Cadillac of rail motorcars, the passenger hi-rail Ford sedan. Usually just the big shots had them, but when they got dinged up we inherited a few.

The thing we never forgot, good times or bad, was the human toll of railroading. Passenger and train crews could distance themselves from it. But when you're working section you know there's blood on every mile of track.

HOSPITAL TRAIN

Few outside the ranks of former railroad employees can appreciate the level of wear and tear on railroad rolling stock during the span of years from World War I to the final collapse of the big railroads in the 1970s and 1980s. Those were years of wartime exigency, depression and recession, and bankruptcy and managerial disarray on some of the mightiest railroads the world had ever seen. On the equipment side, they were years of penny-pinching, deferred maintenance, parts shortages, and extended service life for cars that bordered on museum piece status.

Equipment shortages in World War I mandated continued service of cars from the frontier era. By the time car manufacturing geared up to the demand the war was over. Just as the cars made during World War I were wearing out, the bottomless needs of World War II came along. Old equipment was used until it rusted through or shook apart. Korea and Vietnam also extended the miles on rolling stock used for the shipment of military equipment and ordnance. But by the 1970s the chief pressures on continuance of decrepit material were economic, regulatory, and political.

Many railroads fell into the downward spiral of petitioning for abandonment of lines, cutbacks in service, counterproductive streamlining courtesy of bankruptcy trustees, and machinations over acquisitions and mergers. Many a corporate pillager of the greedy 1980s cut his rapacious teeth on the plunder of railroad assets in the 1970s. Many a railroad worker shook his head in disbelief at business practices that seemed calculated to drive shippers away from rail.

Tom saw all this from the freight conductor's angle. The centerpiece of his tale has to do with a rare and unusual assignment for a conductor. But his audience gathered round him in Ski's Sports Bar in La Crosse, Wisconsin, knows it's about a whole series of questionable decisions made by men in suits in faraway offices.

I took the buyout in the 1980s. I was third-generation Milwaukee Road and couldn't stand the thought of traveling under difficult colors. I'm not saying anything against Soo Line or Canadian Pacific. It's just that those railroads don't have a history in the Mississippi Valley and the Plains. They're jack pine railroads.

The hardest thing I've ever gone through was the unraveling of the Milwaukee Road. It broke my heart when they shut down the western end of the system. That's when I started to draw the hospital trains, which consisted of banged-up and disabled cars headed back to the shops. The western end was full of smashed-up and worn-out cars. They must have had yards full of stuff sitting out there for years in Washington, Idaho, and Montana.

It made me mad every time I saw a rusted and falling-apart car. Especially when I could see it had been in bad shape for years and was given only the maintenance needed to keep it going one more day. It was easy to spot the patch welds, the steel bar and bolts in places where cast metal had cracked, and the jerry-rigged air brake lines. It was a damn shame.

That sort of thing was an embarrassment for the railroad and it hurt business. In railroading, just like all transportation, your equipment is your advertising. All that scrap traveling back from the Pacific Northwest to Milwaukee did as much to hurt the railroad as anything done in Congress, the courts, or the Interstate Commerce Commission. Nothing says you're done for louder than peeling paint and parts falling off.

Don't get me wrong, cars will wear out and sometimes you need to string them together and haul them to the shops for repair. The junk we hauled in 1978, 1979, and 1980 was a far cry from what you have when you bring in cars from a unit coal train derailment or a stretch of retired ore cars being converted to maintenance of way ballast cars. That's different! That's like a group of wounded soldiers or veterans retiring into reserve status. There's pride in that type of hard service. But there's no pride in neglect and deferred maintenance.

Those hospital train runs made me think about these things. Plenty of time to think on a train creeping along at five to ten miles per hour on the main line. We'd pick up a hospital train at St. Paul, Minnesota, and see it down to New Lisbon, Wisconsin, where we'd hand it over to the Portage boys to take into Milwaukee. Then it was clank, thunk, and bang for most of the trip, like embarrassing yourself in your own neighborhood with a dragging muffler. Usually as a conductor you're right at the bay window of the caboose, ready to wave at the kids and wink at the girls. But on some of those hospital trains you wanted to slouch back and pull your hat down over your face. I remember our first big junker in 1978 where a wise-ass teenager at a crossing in Winona said, "Hey, Grandpa, you bringing those back from a Civil War battle?"

That was as clear a reminder as I needed that everyone knew we were goners, even a snot-nosed punk on a bike. It called up the memories of every piece of equipment that was ignored. We would deliver boxcars that had stuck doors to the canneries. So the cannery workers yanked them with comealongs and rammed them with forklifts. At the grain elevators we set out covered hoppers with bottom chutes that wouldn't quite close. Some would lose twenty to thirty tons of corn or wheat on the way to their destination. In the yards the leaky tank cars could just about suffocate you.

It wasn't the carmen or the lack of maintenance capability. I rode with those carmen on hospital trains and I know it pained them to see the cars in such bad shape. They knew it reflected poorly on them. But they were trapped in the cycle that management designed for us. Damn the small shippers, damn the Milwaukee Road's own cars, and damn anything that wasn't a quick tariff producer.

But if a power plant catching one-hundred-car unit trains needed so much as a brake shoe, why hell, a truckload of carmen was dispatched immediately. Replace that shoe pronto, shine the power plant boss's shoes, and kiss his ass too! Not to mention the big bucks that could be pulled in from the routine maintenance of these fleets of unit trains. The car departments really racked up the billings for wheel changes, air brake work, and coupler replacement. So management was not about to let carmen fool with things like hauling a torch out to the sauerkraut cannery in order to heat and reshape a boxcar door track. No money in that!

Going slow in the hospital trains let you see what was happening through this boneheadedness. We looked down many neglected sidings toward businesses we used to serve. We saw grass growing between the ties and trucks delivering lumber, cement, fertilizer, and feed. Plus we saw the new businesses that didn't even bother to build with rail access.

Yup, those scrap pile hospital trains were a moving billboard screaming out to potential customers, "This railroad's history, go with the jet age." We'd limp along knowing that we might have to stop five or six times, knowing that it might take ten to twelve hours to cover the distance. The La Crosse carman-in-charge called them mobile derailments.

Carmen never talked much on a hospital train. They just had worried looks. Usually two rode in the caboose. Sometimes one would ride up front with the hogshead to take care of small problems on the lead end. Spent most of their time in the bay windows scanning the train on the curves, looking for hotboxes and swaying cars with bad side bearings. That and fiddling with their toolboxes and gear like soldiers do with the rifles and packs before a fight. It was never a matter of whether something would go wrong on a hospital train, just when and what.

Usually the luckiest carman was the one who didn't ride the train. He was the one who rode escort in the car department truck, generally following roads near the main line. He carried all the extra tools and parts with him on that truck. Torches, welders, hydraulic jacks, lots of coupler knuckles, big bolts, heavy chains and steel cables, and such. I don't know if the carmen drew straws for the truck or if it went on seniority.

The main problem on a hospital train is that it keeps coming apart. Many have sagging drawbars, smashed-up ends, and cracked yokes and center keys. Some cars have nothing but cracked metal jammed up their centersills and they have to be log-chained to each other. This arrangement works for a short trip for two or three cars to the rip track, but it's a constant accident waiting to happen when it's thirty cars going from Deer Lodge, Montana, to Milwaukee.

That's why a hospital train stops so often. Couplers pull out. Coupler knuckles crack off. Chains break. So the carmen patch it back together and we start again. Often the train breakups come in series. That's often the fault of an engineer with too heavy a touch. On any train you want to take up the slack carefully. But on a hospital train you really have to be gentle.

When the trains come apart you often have air brake problems too. Not just the matter of mating the hoses back together. No, you might have cars in the middle of the train that have no air brake pipes on them. That means long lengths of rubber hose rigged along the side of the train. When the train breaks up from a drawbar problem, there goes the hose too.

They always tried to run these hospital trains during the day and in good weather. But it rarely worked out that way. The carmen always cursed working hospital trains in the rain and in the dark. I know it was hard. But for my money, we should have run them all on rainy nights to spare the Milwaukee Road the humiliation of all that junk that we should have left in the Rockies.

THE MONEY HOLE

Tunnels occupy a unique niche within railroad lore. The juxtaposition of massive equipment with the subterranean world produces a marvel that at once evokes conquest via mechanical engineering and the enduring power of earthly primal forces. Even tunnels in the cheeriest of locales hint at the supernatural and unseen dark forces.

Almost every tunnel in North America has a ghost story. Many an accident and no small amount of foul play in and about tunnels populate the bores with every species of phantom. Yet, scratch the surface and the figurative haunting is fueled by folly and arrogance, and the mood of darkness is the durable shadow cast by greed and callousness.

Railroad tunnels are a major part of the train scene in the Rocky Mountains and the Appalachians. Few think of the Midwest as tunnel territory. Yet, the coulee country and unglaciated driftless uplands of southwest Wisconsin, southeast Minnesota, northeast Iowa, and northwest Illinois offer prime tunnel territory. In rail's golden age, all the major heartland lines dealt with a tunnel or two.

Most are closed today as hazards. A few survive as attractions, such as those one left behind on the Chicago & North Western line from Sparta to Elroy that now serves as a bicycle trail. Elsewhere in the region they are largely forgotten. But don't tell that to Burgess. He might just sit you down in his favorite coffee shop in Galena, Illinois, and give you a lecture.

The real name was the Winston Hole. That's what they called it on the Chicago Great Western when my grandfather come to Jo Daviess County to help dig it. But by the time my father and uncles worked on the CGW they simply called it the Money Hole, on account of the railroad resources fed into it. By my day on the CNW it was just "the hole," with various four-letter prefixes I'll leave to your imagination.

Some say it was the Money Hole that wrecked the CGW. The construction cost was enormous, the equipment and upkeep substantial, and a big daddy jinx just hung over the damn thing. Livestock in cattle cars suffocated in there. Local fools were run over in there. Every disaster railwise within a large radius was blamed on the Money Hole. That includes the big wreck east of the tunnel in 1951 known as the Cornfield Meet. More engines were wrecked in that collision than any other accident on the CGW. Though it didn't occur in the tunnel, everybody referred to it as "the Cornfield Meet by the Winston Hole."

It was real impressive back when it was built in 1888. Well, that's the year it opened after a year of digging. She's 2,400 feet long, one of the longest outside of mountain areas. Plus a ventilation shaft down through the hill. With reinforced portals, to withstand derailments.

The hole was a marvel of its time. At least until they actually used it. You see, it was on what was then the CGW main line. The tunnel was supposed to be a gem of the system. It was supposed to trump the other railroad lines to the west.

Instead it spelled trouble from day one. The ventilation shaft proved inadequate. The heat was so bad that crews suffered burns and heat exhaustion. The air quality was so bad that passengers fainted. So much for modern engineering. All the bragging about the solid construction and the three million bricks lining the bore didn't amount to a hill of beans with those results.

Even way back then, some blamed it on a curse. You see, a worker was killed during construction and there were calls to halt the project that went unheeded. The first death led to a string of misfortunes that included deaths of tunnel crew members in a boardinghouse fire, some killings resulting from crew brawls, and a score of maiming injuries in the hole. So you can see why it was thought to be haunted right up through the time when the CNW closed it in 1972. Curiously, as soon as it closed no one heard anything more about it, except as a hangout for delinquents.

All my family ever did was work on track through the bore. I did a few summers as a young man, until my back gave out. But we knew some of the families more tied to the hole. They were called tunnel operators. There had to be one at either end at all times in those preelectric signal days.

Tunnel operators took the brunt of the grief and bad luck of the hole. My dad said the job made them crazy. It was common for them to walk off at the end of a shift and never be heard from again. Such behavior meant double shifts for those left behind.

Here's how the tunnel operator system worked. There was one man at each station. Winston Station was at the east portal. Rice Station was a mile west of the other portal. Up until automatic block signals they ran a flag or baton system. The CGW called it a staff. The operator at the approach station had to establish the "all clear." Only then would the operator hand the engineer the staff which authorized him to proceed through the hole. The engineer handed the staff to the operator on the other side.

The hole often had two dozen trains a day. That meant that its nasty little ventilation problem had to be addressed. So they built a fan house on the west end. Big fans generated a twenty-five-mile-per-hour wind that cleaned the tunnel air and cooled off the bore. The reputation of the line among passengers improved mightily after that. The fans were diesel powered and cranky. There were many temporary shutdowns for repairs of the fans. Believe me when I say that train crews were none too happy when schedule requirements forced a tunnel run without benefit of the fans. The whole problem ended in 1948 when the CGW switched to diesel locomotives and closed the fan house.

I remember being out there as a boy with my dad. The place had an Alice in Wonderland feel to it, with bug-eyed tunnel operators hiding pints of whiskey at our approach. You could almost imagine that the portal could transport you to another world. Standing there, listening to the strange sounds coming out of the hole, feeling the tunnel wind on your face, and wondering what real and supernatural creatures might lurk in there.

Around the portals themselves, there were plenty of bad omens. Carcasses and skeletons left by predators littered the ground. The hillsides were abuzz with snakes on hot summer days. Operators often carried pistols and shotguns to deal with snakes, not to mention the skunks, rabid possums, and thieving raccoons. There were loads of snakes and big snakes. In the Winston Station I saw rattlesnake skins that must have been five to six feet long, with twelve to fourteen rattle segments. No wonder those operators were buggy.

Dad told me they were most edgy back in World War I. That's when the country was gripped by sabotage hysteria. People became convinced that the hole was a prime target for the Kaiser's evil agents. Part of this dim-witted thinking was the product of the time, with some people expecting to see German submarines on the Mississippi. But part was due to the fact that some of the oldest local blood lines were drawn from peckerwood stock. You know, the great thinkers whose ancestors chased Black Hawk's band in the summer of 1832 so that they could wage heroic battle against starving women and children.

So the local self-anointed militia took it upon themselves to post guards at the hole. I guess they were soon drinking whiskey with the operators, because they came back with reports of strange happenings. One reported that an entire division of Germans was camped on the hill at night. That turned out to be a few local German American farmers drinking home brew and cursing in the mother tongue.

By World War II the mood reversed. Some held out feeble hope that the Germans would bomb the tunnel and level the hill. But seriously, it was clear by then that the hole was a bust and did little to improve the competitive standing of the CGW line. It was just a big expensive lesson in why railroads should avoid hill country.

It's popular to complain about the cost of government projects. How many times have you heard some triple-chinned lardmouth on radio say something about the space program or federal research on cow gas and then claim that we need to run government like business? Well, the Money Hole was conceived and run by business. Run right into the ground, thank you very much. Remember that the next time some slick business boy tells you you're too worked up about NAFTA and the World Trade Organization!

KEY MAN

Control of train movements is now a matter of computer monitoring and electric signals. The day is near when all trains will be tracked and signaled by global positioning systems, communications satellites, fiber optics, and laser signals. Not long ago it was the telegraph operator who ruled rail communications, replacing the early years of hand flags and guesswork. His reign was at least half of the span of the rail age, perhaps more if you count the pockets where the telegraph hung on or continued as a backup system.

The telegraph prevented many of the gross misunderstandings that spurred train accidents in the industrial buildup between the Civil War and World War II. Accidents still occurred, of course, but they were mostly the result of poor judgments and equipment failure rather than lack of communication. As the voices of lonely outposts, railroad telegraphers saved lives on and off the tracks by warnings of blocked tracks, civil disorders, and raging fires.

The survivors of this occupation are few in number, especially those who made a career of it. Here and there I find railroad retirees who spent a few years by the telegraph key until phone lines and electronic signals forced transfers into other rail jobs. I was blessed to talk to one of the original breed in his West Liberty, Iowa, home during his last summer of life. Elson, a World War I veteran, was animated, full of memories, and possessed of great recall of the details of railroad telegraphy.

They called us key men, because of our skill with the telegraph key. It was once an important job and many a station operator, dispatcher, and yardmaster started out as an operator. My old doctor compared the railroad to the human body and said the telegraph operators were the nervous system, sending signals to the eyes, hands, and feet of the railroad. I told him it was just like my body, 'cause the parts don't always listen.

I was an operator for the Chicago, Rock Island & Pacific, or "the Rock," as it was called 'round here. A proud, big railroad that was caught 'twix and 'tween and could never decide if it was a midwestern railroad, a southern railroad, or a western railroad. It really was the railroad that opened Iowa for settlement and it was positioned well for shipment of grain and agricultural machinery. But it had bad luck, squeezed by giants on every side, and the misfortune to service the dust bowl.

It seems to me that the Rock was a pioneer in many things and never got credit for it. Before World War I the Rock was already plenty much switched over to automatic block signals and phone dispatching in the yards. In the years leading up to World War II signalization was extended throughout the system and central traffic control was instituted.

But telegraphy was kept up in many stations as backup and as a way of producing a copy of a train movement order. It hung on off the main lines up until a little after World War II. I did time at Winterset and Montezuma in those days.

I was trained by the old-timers, mostly old Mr. Desmond from Iowa Falls. He was a stickler for the rules, made us memorize them by number. During most of those years there were twenty-one rules for train movement by telegraph. Desmond pounded them into the new men. I don't remember all the numbers, but I think I know them by order of importance.

All orders are to be authorized by train dispatchers. All special orders are to be conveyed to the engineer and conductor. All orders not understood by an operator must be repeated and clarified. All orders transmitted to two or more stations must be addressed first to the operator holding the train and then to the stations in order of ranking of train priority.

Orders must be made on manifold carbon paper, with enough copies for the engineer, the conductor, the operator, and the dispatcher file. Orders must be written in full and contain no abbreviations except number codes and letters authorized in the operator's manual. Orders requiring an answer must be endorsed and time of endorsement logged by the conductor, with copy conveyed to the engineer. Any order ending with the letters RX must be repeated exactly by the receiving operator back to the dispatcher for confirmation.

Operators are required to read aloud to conductors all orders addressed to them affecting the movement of their trains. Duty operators must make relief operators acknowledge logging and receipt of all orders still in effect. Operators must display signal requiring train stops. Operators must ensure prompt delivery of orders.

Orders to hold a train require immediate display of the red signal and immediate response to the dispatcher that the signal is out. After delivery of orders the signal must be taken in. If the red signal is out and a train arrives for which there are no orders, the operator must provide clearance to the conductor on appropriate forms and allow the train to proceed. Orders concerning track obstructions, inadequacy of water supply, and other conditions of concern to trainmen require the operator to obtain the conductor's signature.

Operators will acknowledge orders with reply indicating order number, station, and initials. Orders addressed to more than one train must be given to each and endorsed by each. Orders indicating train order among several trains must be coded "10," followed by the number of trains. Orders concerning train order will be given on copies to the conductors indicating the movement order, thus: 10-1, 10-2, et cetera. All orders shall be numbered consecutively for each day, starting with 1 at midnight.

Those were the standing orders. There were other rules for special circumstances. Things like train abandonment, work trains, meetings of trains to exchange orders, emergency conditions, and countermanding of prior orders. All of these conditions had special forms and had to be sent in specific message style. The forms for such conditions were code lettered and were in an operator's manual.

All this passed from the scene as the Rock modernized. By the time I retired hardly anyone remembered the standing orders and special forms. Most of the telegraph agents I knew became clerks and agents, although some moved up into management. The bosses knew that if you could handle train orders you pretty much understood railroading and could handle whatever came your way.

Some of our Rock Island operators had one more brush with glory. In World War II a bunch of us were pulled into the military training programs to show army and navy radio instructors how to train recruits in telegraph skills and message transcription. Some went into the military and ran communication stations. We heard it was a Rock Island telegrapher who sat in the flagship radio room and sorted the message traffic at the Battle of Midway.

Key men had their own legends and heroes. There were always stories about telegraph operators who wired ahead to the next town about prairie fires whipping toward unsuspecting people. There were railroad telegraphers who let outside help know that towns had been flattened by tornadoes. There were many tales about operators keeping each other alert, where a station operator might just have a hunch that a tower operator was dozing and might need a little poke over the line before another railroad's train ran a crossing.

It all changed and we were just a little bit of history. But I don't have many regrets. Well, maybe one. I wished the Rock would have merged with the Union Pacific in 1974. It would have kept things going better here in Iowa.

SHOP CHICKS

More than three decades passed between the World War II days when women worked on the railroads and the times when they reappeared in modest numbers. While the absence of women was not always the result of exclusionary or discriminatory policies, the railroads certainly were "boys' clubs." Women were rarely in a position to take advantage of the tavern and hardware store networks that might lead to a job referral.

Honesty compels an admission that those networks screened women out by direct and indirect means. It often occurred that the section crew was the "entry

*level" for the railroads, hard and dirty work that drew few women applicants
and yet served as a testing ground for railroad commitment. Smaller yards and
facilities in rural areas often acted as "feeders" for workers throughout a particular
rail system, leaning toward part-time farmers and loggers who had the patience to
build up seniority through years of seasonal layoffs.*

*Even the time-honored rail referral system of family seldom benefited
women. Few fathers, brothers, uncles, and cousins were likely to mention job
openings to female relatives. Paternalism figured largely in this process; the desire
to protect was often cited by elder railroaders who were otherwise committed to
workplace equity. Some old-timers worried themselves over issues like the prevalence
of foul language and the casual answering of nature's call in rail yards. Others
adopted the attitude that a woman on the railroad was taking a job away from
a male head of household.*

*When the general shifts in society hit the railroads in the 1970s, the
patriarchy was in for many shocks. The graybeards discovered that many among
this new generation of women were accustomed to profane language and creative
in its exercise. It also turned out that few were delicate about bodily processes.
But perhaps the biggest culture shock came with the recognition that the new
generation of women railroaders had many single mothers whose need for the
paycheck was as pressing as any man's.*

*Wanda was part of that wave of the 1970s. She didn't get to stay in rail-
roading, but she did develop an affinity for the transportation industry. I caught
up with her at a South Beloit, Illinois, truck stop, where she was waiting to take
on fuel and coffee.*

They called us shop chicks in Milwaukee, and we really hated it back
then. It was definitely an uncool word in the late 1970s. Women friends
didn't use it among themselves like younger women might today. Back
then there were men who used the words just to get a reaction out of us.

A whole group of us came into the Milwaukee Shops in 1978. There
were maybe a dozen of us at first. Four of us lasted into the next year, and
each year, up through 1980, they hired five to ten women. Only a couple
others hung in as long as those of us in the original group.

I came in as a carman welder. I had the welding training through
technical school. When I came up to Milwaukee to live with my aunt I worked
in a candy factory and then got laid off. When the unemployment payments
were about to run out I had to find something so I could support my two
boys. The Job Service office in Milwaukee sent me down for the opening,
but I could tell the man at Job Service didn't think I could pass the shop
welding test or make much of an impression in an interview.

His attitude was clear, so I could read his mind. It was right on his face what he was thinking: big colored gal with a scar on her face and too stupid to know the difference between cows and cabooses. Lucky for me the car shop foreman didn't think like that. He said right off that I have big hands for a gal and he was thinking that he wouldn't have trouble with a plain-looking hefty gal.

Working in the shops was a new experience for me. My experience with white people was kind of limited, mostly teachers and police. I learned there were all kinds of white people with all kinds of ideas and ways of treating other people. I met Belgians, Danes, and Bohemians and other groups I never heard of before.

What surprised me the most was the white country folks. If a white man was to come up and offer me a smoke or sit down aside me at lunch, it was usually a farm boy from western Wisconsin or Iowa. Some of them had never met a black woman before. The only thing most of them knew about minorities came from sports or the military. They were real good workers too and willing to show new employees how to do things.

It was the first time I ever had men for friends. The two I was closest to were an odd pair. There was Mark, a former Amish man who ran away to join the army, and Billy, a Mandan Indian who did a few years in North Dakota prisons. Mark helped me with my welding, while Billy taught me pipe work and metal bending.

More importantly, they taught me about the Milwaukee Road and railroads in general. See, for those of us who came because Job Service sent us, there were a lot of lessons to learn. You could treat a job in the shops like it was on an assembly line or you could act like you were part of a team moving things across the country. I had no idea that so many men lived and breathed railroading. Not all of them in the shops, of course, there was plenty of dead wood in there too. But it was the first place I ever met people who looked forward to work.

There were freight carmen welders and freight carmen mechanics in the shops who worked all of the country. The ones who had worked in the yards and out on the wrecks took a lot of pride in fixing cars and sending them out the door. As the end of the Milwaukee Road got closer we had a lot of no-accounts who didn't share that view. We had a core that hid in the john all day. It was the only place I ever worked where men spent a longer time in the bathroom than women.

The place was run real goofy, too. You got the idea that those in charge didn't have a clue about what they were doing. There were people who didn't really have a job or anything to do. Just about the most dangerous place on Earth to work. I saw my share carried out, including one guy squashed like a bug when the overhead crane went crazy. We walked out that day.

Our little core of women stuck together through those last years of the shops. We were all quite different and quite a few of them had been college girls. Most of the white girls came out of college and were radicals always talking politics. Nobody had a clue on what they was saying, stuff about liberation in Africa and revolution in Central America. It's amazing how most of those women became college professors, except for one Mexican woman and a couple of South Milwaukee Polish women.

One of those Polish girls got me tied into trucking through an uncle. She took it up too, but I haven't seen her for years. Funny how we started out hauling piggyback trailers off of railroad cars. I like that feeling of being part of moving what needs to be moved. I know I wouldn't have learned that without my time in the shops.

PART THREE
Fellow Travelers

Many of us still thrill to the call of "all aboard," even when it is only an echo of a youthful memory. The comings and goings of trains have touched us as a people since their invention. Riding, watching, and pondering trains have all left marks on our culture and our souls. Passengers may be affluent, of modest means, accidental, and even illicit. Observers may have trained eyes or warm familiarity. They are united in fraternity when the conversation turns to trains. They cannot stop talking about them.

DROVER'S CABOOSE

Midwest railroading had many features that built up its standing as America's crossroads of commerce. Minerals from the West, finished goods from the East, timber from the North, and coal and textiles from the South all criss crossed the great yards of Chicago, Milwaukee, St. Paul, Omaha, Kansas City, and St. Louis. But from the 1870s to the 1970s one mainstay of the rail freight trade was livestock shipment.

The transport of live cargo caused the evolution of an odd occupation associated with heartland railroading, that of train drover. Drovers were one part cowboy, one part herdsman, and one part longshoreman or warehouseman. The job involved driving livestock to the railroad, sorting them at the railhead, loading them for shipment, feeding and watering them during the trip, and unloading them at the destination. Throw in the need for minor veterinary care, repair of decrepit livestock cars, and cooking en route and you are talking about a sturdy breed.

The train drover's job evolved out of the great cattle drives of the post–Civil War era. The thousand-mile drives down from Montana and up from Texas were gradually whittled down to fifty- and one-hundred-mile drives as rail penetrated farther and farther into the grasslands of the Great Plains. But the big slaughter-houses were still back in the Midwest, and a load of steers required more care than a hopper car of gravel. Thus the train drover gained his niche.

Eventually train droving gave rise to a variety of specialized rolling stock and accommodations. Sometimes drovers bunked in special baggage cars with their saddle horses. In the early days they even slept under tarps on flatcars. But the highest form of drover amenity devised by the railroad design engineers was the drover's caboose. It was bunkhouse, tack room, and dining car rolled into one.

Dan, survivor of a long line of train drovers, recalls the tricks of the trade as he train watches with a grandson in their hometown of Sioux City, Iowa. The sounds and sights of modern rail movements evoke the smells and load shifts of the long gone livestock cars. Dan transports us back to that time.

Those days of cows on the trains are gone. The shipments mostly were done by the 1970s. The semis and interstates took care of that. Well, the feedlotting and slaughtering industries had a hand in it too.

But for a good long while you were likely to see livestock trains every day. Here in Sioux City, up in Sioux Falls, and down in Council Bluffs, the whole of the northern plains spilled their livestock through like the leaks in a big spring ice jam about to bust. Hard to imagine that at one time every Midwest rail yard had the bellowing of animals and the whiff of manure tacked on to all the other chaos a train operation throws at the senses.

Our family had a hand in the livestock shipping deal. Yep, we had a baker's dozen or more train drovers in the family tree. I'm the last of them, and like land, they ain't making no more.

Train drovers came in as many subspecies as pigeons. There was the matter of who they worked for. Only a handful were actual railroad employees. Some of the railroads fiddled with drover service as an add-on to shipment tariffs, but it was kind of a boondoggle. One or two had cattle subsidiaries coming out of those land grant swindles they pulled in the early days.

But most train drovers were private employees, though I heard tell of government train drovers back in the First Big One and before that, U.S. army cavalry train drovers. The majority worked for ranchers, cattle brokers, stockyards, or meatpackers. But you had some contract train droving crews too. And all sorts of hybrids like joint ventures, co-op, and droving on shares.

The drover trade descended right out of prehistoric time, when nomads pushed their livestock to market to buy supplies, hootch, and wives. Sure, it evolved and by the time of the Old West they had transmuted into that peculiar creature known popularly as the cowboy. Though to a man, that class of *homo erectus* referred to themselves as ranch hands.

The cowboy mutated into the train drover on that glorious day when those long drives from Billings, Montana, to Omaha, Nebraska, by way of Sheridan, Wyoming, and the North Platte River ran into the ribbons of steel poking west. Train tracks eventually made it to Rapid City, South Dakota, and Scottsbluff and North Platte in Nebraska. It cut the drives in half. So, not to be denied their blowout in the big towns, the cowboys rode the train the rest of the way.

The first train drovers rode on top of the cattle cars. Some fatalities and the increase in winter shipments took care of that. So they were moved into the mail express car. But they were eventually crowded out by parcel freight. Then they were given passes to attached passenger coaches. The early trains were almost always combines of freight and passengers, you know. But the passengers didn't like the smell, profanity, and leering eyes of the train drovers. In the end they were kicked into the cabooses.

That was the beginning of a long, if uneasy, love affair between drovers and trains. The start of the relationship was a bit rocky. Cabooses were very small in those days. Conductors and brakemen didn't much care for extra company in those tight quarters. Plus you had the apples and oranges in their situations. Train crewmen changed in different sections. Heck, the cars themselves might be transferred to a different railroad. But train drovers stayed with the animals until the destination.

If the railroads had not been so busy growing, going bankrupt, and buying each other up in those days, the section crew bunkcar might have evolved sooner and lent itself to drover service. But track gangs in those days were encamped in tent or shanty cities out in virgin territory.

The problem was solved by building drover cabooses. First, by taking all kinds of other cars, throwing some bunks in, slapping some red paint on, and sticking them on the end of the train. But they were neither fish nor fowl, and neither crews nor drovers were entirely happy.

So the car builders went to work on the problem. In those days the mechanical trades of the railroad were filled with men of a mystical quality. They traced their lineage back to the builders of cathedrals and pyramids. Their discussions were candlelit lodge ceremonies and most of their leaders were freemasons. Out of the dim car shops and this stew of secret knowledge and sworn oaths came the drover's caboose.

The drover's caboose was the stretch limousine of cabooses. They were long and, by work equipment standards, they were luxurious. They went way past any cowboy notions of comfort. Instead of the ranch water trough for personal hygiene, there were honest to goodness sinks. Instead of drafty outhouses with splintery planks, there was a rock solid water closet with a smooth-seated toilet.

These cabooses were roomy too. They came in four- and six-bunk varieties. They had cookstoves and pantry space. Many had storage areas for saddles, blankets, and bridles. There were almost as many windows as a passenger coach, and a few even had curtains. Here and there, you might even find a drover caboose with an icebox.

Don't get me started on the debate about who had the best drover cabooses. Our family was loyal to the Great Northern. That road kept its cabooses clean and well maintained. It's true Milwaukee Road built some beauties, but they banged them up pretty good loaning them out for yard work and work trains. Chicago & North Western had some nice ones, but you couldn't count on one being like the next.

In a way, the drover caboose design wasn't that important, except in how it shaped drover caboose culture. That's right, culture. It was a slice of life never seen before or since.

Understand that I'm talking about real drovers, cattle drovers. Technically you had train drovers dealing with all kinds of livestock. But it was cattle that were moved with frequency and in numbers by real cowhands. The other animal cargoes didn't have the aura of beef on the hoof.

We didn't look down on horse drovers, be they handling saddle horses, draft horses, or range mustangs from out west. But we never saw that as real work. A real drover would take a hundred-car train of horses from Tijuana to Nova Scotia for a vacation.

Other critters? That's a monkey of a different hue. There was a time when plenty of sheep were moved by rail. Sheep are too damn sensitive. They drop over dead if someone says an unkind word. We called sheep drovers things like sheepherds, shepturds, shitherds, and some downright insulting things.

Pigs? That was even worse. You could smell a hog handler clear across a forty-track yard. Nobody wanted to use a drover caboose after a hog run. We called those fellows the pork patrol, oinkers, and pig pushers. We ribbed them pretty hard.

Other animals could occasionally get shipped by train. Herds of goats, buffalo, and laboratory animals, but I never saw them. With poultry the water and feed were right in the car so there was no off and on the cars every twelve hours like with beef.

So the camaraderie of the drover caboose was really just a cowhand's thing. It was a closed circle and outsiders rarely got a glimpse of the life. Maybe you could compare it to some things. Like life for a professional firefighter at the fire station. Or a bunch of guys on a hunting trip, living in a little cabin. Or even sailors at sea.

It just captivated me as a young fellow. Got my start early. Started train droving at fifteen years old. I was big for my age and the Second Big One was raging in Europe and the Pacific. They weren't too fussy about manpower and had soldiers to feed.

I was pretty full of myself. Out of school for the summer. Chance to see Montana. Following in my dad's and granddad's footsteps and all. And at an unusual time. The West was sure different in those days. Hardly any young men around. Everything was being done by old men, gimpy guys, boys, and women. If you could throw a bale of hay you were treated like Paul Bunyan himself.

And the women! Geez, were the women out and about. And lonely. Let me tell you, a young man could get quite an education in those little towns in those days. Did we ever talk about it in those cabooses.

Caboose talk. That's what train drovers called anything off-color, exaggerated, or confidential among men. Caboose talk happened in the drover caboose just about any time under any circumstance. But some things just primed it. Card playing and whiskey drinking. Mealtime eating and coffee sipping. And just looking out the windows in the long empty stretches.

It was odd talk in many ways. At least in my time. Remember, this was during the Second Big One. So it was old weathered cowboys and peach fuzz teenagers talking to each other. Almost like some long ago tribe where the battle-crippled geezers guarded the village with a complement of boys, while the able-bodied stalked the enemy over the next hill.

Boy virgins were coached on the technical aspects of their first romantic encounters. New train drovers were given the short course on telling one end of the cow from the other. Information about amorous ladies in certain railroad towns was exchanged. Nasty rumors about big butt conductors were cheerfully circulated. And train-droving stories were told.

Real legends some of them. Mostly about the early drovers and the cowboy myths behind them. A good train drover story always managed to throw in a couple Indian attacks, a Civil War battle, a mountain man brawl, a painted saloon girl, a rancher's pure daughter, a crooked banker, a corrupt sheriff, a greedy railroad executive, and, of course, a heroic train drover as tough as a marine and as upright as a Canadian mountie.

I'm not bragging or nothing, but we had quite a few of these stories in our family. It's even said that we had a great uncle who was a legendary train drover. I haven't figured out the blood tie. Could be that he was just a friendly old-timer who picked up the "uncle" label. But we sure had the Uncle Bill stories.

Uncle Bill was known in every drover caboose north of Kansas City. He was the patron saint of drovers in the Midwest and northern plains. South of that, drovers spit at the mention of him. Uncle Bill apparently had a lot of gun notches from Reb guerrillas he permanently pacified in Kansas and Missouri. Guess he had a checkered past too. Something about name changes and warrants out on him.

Uncle Bill was the model train drover though. I guess he saw the trade through its big days from the Civil War to the First Big One. He set the standard. Train drover behavior was measured by what Uncle Bill said and did.

This was a point of pride for our family, but also a burden. When a snake-mean old train drover would find out we were Uncle Bill's nephews, he would like as not turn quiet and respectful. Old-timers acted fatherly toward us and our caboose colds were nursed and our cattle pen wounds tended with a love beyond Florence Nightingale's.

It could change real quick though. If the veteran drovers thought we weren't up to the task at hand, they would give us a disgusted look and say something like, "You're never gonna measure up to Uncle Bill." Or, "Your mama didn't get the same seed that sprouted Uncle Bill, maybe you're from the milkman." And stuff worse than that.

I guess I think that the drover's caboose deserves its own glorified spot in the lore of livestock country. As a place where men engaged life, and loved it with enthusiasm and friendship, it ranks right up with the fishing cabin, the hunting lodge, the logger's bunkhouse, the naval seaman's quarters, or the soldier's tent. It was a campfire, tavern, and church on steel wheels.

Anybody who ever train droved won't ever forget those cabooses. They won't forget the wild characters, wise men, droll cowboy humorists, and hard-as-nails tough guys. They won't soon forget the prairie sunsets, the friendly small town people, the crusty train crews, and the big stockyards. Add that on to all the old stories of Uncle Bill and his breed—the long cattle drives, the roping and branding, the sleeping under the stars—and you have as good a slice of America as you can find.

I made only a few runs after I came back from the Korean War, so my experience was really one of my boyhood. Train drover, marine, and insurance agent—all before I was 25 years old. But my memories of those drover's cabooses are as clear as a Chinese bugle before a Korean winter attack. I'd love to have one of those cabooses to restore.

Or better yet, use a drover caboose like Uncle Bill did. The story has it that he was an old man when he found an abandoned one in a bitter storm. He passed on in the shelter of that drover caboose. It was on a siding near the old livestock barns and holding pens right here in Sioux City. He was buried right there. The old steam trains blew the whistle when they passed by the spot.

As the story goes, this happened in the time of a big epidemic. So they buried him quick. Cut the brake rods and pin lifters right off that caboose, lifted that car right off the wheel trucks and center sills, and placed it in a long trench where they put diseased cattle. They buried him all right. Buried him as he lived—in a drover caboose.

TATER FRATERS

When one thinks of rail shipment of commodities today, the unit trains of coal immediately come to mind. But there was a time, not long ago, when commodity shipments meant foodstuffs and other agricultural products that might be traded in Chicago. Few would have guessed that the mainstays of cattle, sugar beets, and grain would soon be replaced by auto racks and containerized freight.

Throughout the Midwest there were specialized cars and tailored cars for virtually every type of food and fiber yielded up by the land. Go to Wisconsin's central sands bog country and some will remember rail-shipping cranberries. In the southern reaches of Iowa there were once pecan shipments. Small town canneries invariably had their sidings on which to load their bounties of canned peas, sweet corn, pickles, and sauerkraut.

Minnesota had its "tater fraters," or potato freight cars. While not as famed as the citrus trains from Florida and California, the tater fraters brought many a smile to farmers and former farm boys. There was a measure of comfort, no, smugness, to be derived from seeing the humble tubers riding in state-of-the-art cars. For country folks weaned with the up-close and personal farming of bending over in fields of soil so loose it pushed up between toes, it was vindication of sorts. It was almost as good as seeing a circus train or a string of Schlitz Brewery cars.

Rodney earned his crop-shipping stripes in service of growers cooperatives in the old Nonpartisan League strongholds of North Dakota. Then came the call to potato country. He didn't know then that the lowly potato would take him on a journey from hardscrabble farm product brokering to a big well-appointed house in an exclusive Twin Cities suburb.

When I was offered the position, I never dreamed that rail-shipping potatoes would make me a rich man. It sure didn't start out that way. When I first went to Minnesota's Red River Valley almost the entire production was going to the government, mostly to military bases. But it was something that the deferred and 4-Fs among us could do and feel a bit better about not going into uniform.

Like everything in that war, the shipments were frantic and not so well planned. As for cars, we took what we got. There were never enough cars in World War II to ship everything or haul anybody. We shoveled and forked taters into boxcars still stinking with gone-bad mutton, placing slats across the doorway until the taters were inches from the top. We bagged taters and used fire brigade relays to load them into open gondolas and hopper cars in good weather. Give us a chance and we'd even load taters into a cattle car and never mind the cleaning up after the former occupants. In war it was always "get it out of here, it's the problem of the next guy down the road."

It stayed that way for a bit after the war. Europe had not recovered and could use every potato we could spare. So we had big loads going all the way to New York, transshipped from Great Northern to Pennsylvania Railroad, New York Central, and Baltimore & Ohio. You have to remember that the Great Lakes weren't yet open to the Atlantic.

In 1946 and 1947 my curiosity got the better of me and I traveled out to the coastal ports to see how the taters were handled. It wasn't a pretty picture. The cold weather shipments were freezing and the hot weather shipments had problems with rot. Taters are pretty resilient critters, but they'll take only so much abuse. The whole experience put notions in the back of my head.

The real immediate lessons of my trip had to do with loading and unloading. Even back in Minnesota some processors were starting to experiment with conveyors, roller panels, pallets, and lifts. On New York's docks I saw whole new methods playing out. On some of the wharves you could see the ancient method of boom and cargo net, modernized only by motorized winch. But here and there you could see technology rearing its head, escalator-style ramps, bins on rollers, and conveyors of all shapes and designs.

When I got back to Minnesota I took up the matter with my local representative of the Great Northern. He said he'd pass the information along. I thought that would be the end of it because, face it, corporate hierarchies are where ideas go to die. But dang if I didn't get a call from

St. Paul a few days later. He said they were toying with some ideas along similar lines and asked would I come down for a meeting.

I most certainly did. It was probably the most important trip of my life, certainly the most profitable. I found a railroad on the brink of major changes in how it handled agricultural products. Would I accompany them on a trip to California to look at some new methods in the produce and citrus areas? You bet.

What we found were some former defense contractors looking for uses of idle facilities and stockpiled materials. We watched and we listened, but back in the hotel at night I pointed out how their loading and car designs were still awkward and on too small a scale. We could do better, I insisted.

When we got back to St. Paul we put a design team together. We brought in some agricultural equipment designers, men familiar with the mechanics of silo fillers, hay bale conveyors, and such. We consulted car shop mechanical engineers. We even consulted investment men who might be considered the forerunners of marketing analysts, to determine what the American consumer wanted, where could it be grown, and where must it be shipped.

We were very secretive. The shipper business could be quite competitive and even areas served by one line would want the pride of the latest technology. Plus those of us in this little cabal knew that our advance information was quite valuable. We were to be partners in patents and could expect that a little bit invested here and there in land and processing facilities in the target areas would yield a tidy pile. Yes, it did.

The details of these things took some years to work out. Experimentation and the lessons of practical application consumed time. Then there was the delicate matter of Great Northern's relationship with its subsidiary Western Fruit Express. We wished them to remain a good little subsidiary, docile and ignorant of what lay ahead. Not that we weren't willing to enrich them. In fact, we contrived to test many new systems on their service areas in the expanding produce areas in the valleys of the Cascades.

We were also mindful of the picayune notions of the antitrust laws that were operative in those days and the attendant ICC glumness concerning interrailroad entanglements. But to make this work, we really needed coordination of the major shippers and standardization of equipment. So we brought in more silent partners, and the outgrowth was an informal partnership of rail executives, produce express subsidiaries, buyers, and brokers. When we had this all figured out, we contrived to reap further reward by keeping the fabrication of equipment controlled by our tight circle. So everything needed for the new era of produce shipping was to come out of a plant jointly owned by Western Fruit Express, Fruit Growers Express, and Burlington Refrigeration Express.

The most colorful product of this venture was the Western Fruit Tater Frater. They were seen zooming by on every line in America and were, for a time, as much a part of the rail landscape as the cars of Oscar Mayer and Hormel. Western Fruit and GN actually received fan mail and requests for Tater Frater photos from boys across the country.

The designs went through several configurations and a few paint schemes fell by the wayside. But basically what we ended up with was an all-steel car of eighty-ton capacity, sixty-two feet long. Though not overwhelming by today's standards it was a behemoth of its day. It was specifically built and doored for conveyor loading and unloading, using equipment that we designed.

We also incorporated the lessons of California into the new design. Tater shippers of yore can tell you about many cars of taters turning to mush and mold as they cooked on sidings in California and Texas. So we went with state-of-the-art cooling systems, top-of-the-line Detroit diesel engines for power, and the premier York system for refrigeration. I daresay a better refrigerator car has never been built.

As if fortune had not shined on me enough, I was able to broker the Old Dutch deal, Old Dutch being that beloved potato chip of the Midwest. The Red River Valley became the source of taters for Old Dutch. The company was an enthusiastic user of our unloading system. And at any given time a considerable portion of the Tater Frater fleet might be seen at their St. Paul potato chip plant.

I made out very well. Maybe they were just taters. But they were gold to me.

KING OLE: HOBO BOSS OF THE MIDWEST

Railroaders concede a love-hate relationship with the transients who have illicitly ridden the rails since the earliest days of train travel. The label hobo is the catchall for various names, pejoratives, and downright unprintable epithets. But even the most biased train jockeys differentiate between the rough tramp elements and those hobos who possess class and style.

Train crews and yard workers often had confrontations with hobos, with tales of hobo-initiated theft and intimidation not uncommon. Railroad police, of course, had the most negative stereotypes of hobos, and many police saw in each impoverished transient a potential felon. On the other hand, the "grease and cinders crafts"—the section crews, the carmen, the engine oilers, and roundhouse laborers—often exhibited empathy toward those hobos they sensed were down on their luck through no fault of their own.

The one thing that is not often found among railroaders is a personal or family connection to a hobo. George won't broadcast his blood tie to a famous hobo, but the former Great Northern tower man and depot clerk will confess the

relationship as long as the family name is kept out of it. The salvaged boxcar
siding in the den of his St. Paul, Minnesota, home tells a tale of his past work-
life and his retirement hobby of woodworking. The black-stenciled Great Northern
goat emblem almost seems to be laughing at the family secret.

It's true, King Ole was a relative. Great-uncle I guess, on Dad's side. So that puts the obvious smack-dab in the middle of the table. He was as Norwegian as a kippered herring.

Now about this "king" thing. There's no connection between our family and the current royal house of Norway. King Ole never made such a claim, he just failed to correct such assumptions. In his old age he laughed at a newspaper write-up that referred to him as a pretender to the Oslo throne.

It was just one of the many things that embarrassed the family. It was bad enough to be a hobo in a solid railroad family, but to put on airs and act a bit like a dandy, well, that violated our workingman's code. It was almost as bad as having your flesh and blood prancing around as a Soo Line superintendent or working on some toy railroad like the Rock Island. But truth be known, those skeletons are also in our family closet.

The irksome thing is, Ole could have had a job on the railroad. Our family was born to it. Rails for bones, journal box oil in our veins, and tough as a creosoted tie from the neck up. Ole was bright and capable, filled with book smarts and rail yard smarts. And he was a hard worker when he needed a grubstake.

But Ole was a true hobo in that he'd rather cut off all his fingers with a rusty cornknife than spend time under the supervision of a boss. Many a hobo in the old days would do fieldwork on a farm for meals and a little pocket change. They'd work until sweat ran down their backsides. It was the idea of an overseer they couldn't abide. A true 'bo thinks of us working stiffs as a bunch of peckerheaded slaves.

So what was the relationship of hobos to the railroads? Were they parasites and lurking thieves? Or were they heart-of-gold travelers who just never found the end of the rainbow? The truth or truths, as always, is both and a mix of both. Hobos defy description as a group unless you look at an overarching character like Ole, someone who represents a wide swath of history.

Ole himself told me, when I was but a pup, that hobos come in several breeds and that changes in railroading cause evolution among the breeds. Now we're talking about an old fellow here that was born only a decade after the Civil War and rode the freights up into the Depression and World War II. So you wouldn't be blowing smoke up the bunghole to say that he saw railroading and hoboing at their high-water marks.

His thumbnail history of hoboing was simple. In the times of the primitive trains a hobo was a fellow who couldn't afford to pay for a ticket and rode anyhow. Right after the Civil War the hobos were disabled veterans, unemployed immigrants, freed slaves, and cowboys—all shifting around trying to find work. Then came the opening up of the whole country in the 1890s. The hobo element was young then, with flair, and a sense of adventure. According to Ole, you could meet young 'bos with sooty faces who would bet the family jewels that they'd become millionaires. And some of them did. In higher percentages than the general population.

This was Ole's heyday. He had a jump on it, starting at age eleven as a big lad too stubborn for a widowed mother to control. His dad a loco-motive fireman killed by a boiler explosion, Ole had a strange relationship to the rail industry. Not vengeful, as you might suspect, but reverential and deep. Railroading at the time represented the muscle of a new nation. It tied together all the other economic bones of mining, lumbering, manu-facturing, and agriculture. It was where the action was—from scandal and political corruption to bloody strikes.

Ole ranged the heartland of America. The grain mills of Minneapolis to the stockyards of Kansas City and Chicago. From the copper holes of the Upper Peninsula to the iron ranges of Minnesota to the coal pits of Illinois. Rode all the big names—Burlington, Chicago & North Western, Illinois Central, Milwaukee Road, and, of course, Great Northern. Not to mention the little puddle-jumping roads like Green Bay and Western.

All and all, the best territory in the world for hobos. Some of the Chicago yards were rough, but none of the twenty-four-hour-a-day meanness of New York, or Los Angels after the dust bowl. Not to mention how hobos just disappeared in places like Nashville and Atlanta—gator food, I guess.

Ole presided over a gentle kingdom that fit his Norwegian genes. He would often write a letter to a populist newspaper editor or settlement house ladies to bring attention to bad treatment of rail tramps. He had no real authority, but he did command respect from all the hobo factions and most of the hands-on railroaders.

His connection to the railworkers was not just a matter of our family history. Ole knew enough about railroading to be of service and, in a way, earn his fare. He knew a defective coupler or missing brake shoe when he saw it. He often left little notes to the mechanic-in-charge at the carman's shed in yards he passed through. He told the problem, the car number, and the yard track number. He had a network of hobos that turned in reports of bad switches, defective signals, and cracked trestle beams.

Even when the hobos became more radical in the days before World War I, he worked to keep the peace and protect life and limb. He helped delay the passage of strikebreakers to sites of labor unrest. He kept the worst red hotheads away from the police lines. He sent telegraphs to pastors in city missions to warn if vigilantes down the line were stirring up antihobo violence.

Yet I have to admit that Ole was more than a saintly hobo. If that was all he was remembered for, my family would be proud to claim him. No, he was remembered for his many dubious achievements as con man, huckster, grifter, gigolo, and purveyor of the weird and grotesque. That's where the title "king" came from.

You couldn't begin to imagine the stunts and feats and contests he staged. Everything that you can think of under the sun that was tasteless and likely to offend the guardians of public morals. Every gross body function and obscene act was just another competitive opportunity.

Let's see, what are some of the famous ones? For starters, there was the hundred hobos standing up on top of boxcars taking a leak as they chugged past a church picnic in Minnesota, laughing at the fainting ladies. And then there was the time he packed a Legion Hall with the smelliest and filthiest hobos he could round up for the speeches of politicians calling for tougher vagrancy laws.

In Iowa, they remember him for the Great American Fart Off. That was a contest he organized along with a big hobo jungle bean feed. It was an explosive event attended by hobos and railroaders. The brakemen in our family said the engineers did pretty well in the competition. You can guess the categories—the loudest, the foulest, best musical tune, and so forth.

This gives you an idea about the specifics of his various snot-blowing, mucus-hawking, and booger-flicking matches. Not to mention the milder pursuits of booze-chugging, tripe-gorging, and various and sundry pie and watermelon contests. Whatever it was, it had to be on a grand scale.

So it was even for his funeral. In a way, that was the final insult for the family, having to elbow their way through the great unwashed to pay their last respects. He had left strange last requests about his funeral arrangements that further offended sensibilities. He was embalmed sitting upright, on a commode prettied up to be a throne, big belly hanging over a leopard skin loincloth, wearing a necklace of bull testicles, and a big stogie in his mouth.

But it was quite a party. Plenty of music, with jugs, saws, banjos, squeezeboxes, and washtub fiddles. Plenty of food, with stew in a big cauldron, tripe, and Rocky Mountain oysters. All timed to a Great Northern freight whistling through three nearby crossings.

STEAMING ORE

Many a love affair with trains started with a nonrailroad job that placed its holder in proximity to railroad equipment. This was especially true in the joint heyday of railroading and heavy industry. The trains came, quite literally, right into the hearts of foundries, mills, and mines. The sounds of the locomotives and the bustle of sidings were as much a part of working life in a factory district as smokestacks and quitting time whistles.

It is true that some major industries rated their own locomotives and switching crews. Some bulk commodity producers went from obscure names to keystone status in huge raw material conglomerates by virtue of a logo or slogan on a fleet of private freight cars seen throughout North America. Train watchers took delight in spotting colorful refrigerated meat cars, dusty hoppers of grain and flour, flats of mill fresh I-beams and pipe, and bulkheads stacked sky high with fragrant new cut lumber.

A faceless and unknowledged army of workers toiled in or about these cars in hundreds of industries. Rail cousins to warehousemen and stevedores, these were the laborers who loaded, unloaded, and serviced the cars in dozens of different ways. They were the unsung hands and backs that did the work now done mostly by equipment and technology. They loaded the hundred-pound sacks of animal feed, they unloaded the crates of canned peas, and they rolled beer barrels up ramps. They swept and fumigated the boxcars, loaded ice, patched floor holes, and refueled compressor engines. They wrestled with balky hopper hatches, plugged leaky tanks, rehung bent boxcar doors, and flagged bad cars for the rail crews.

These are the forgotten workers of the rail world, the laborers with tools of the trade no more complex than short-handled scoop shovels, leather gloves, baling hooks, and pry bars. This is their story, told by one of their number, in one upper Midwest industry. Gabe lives just outside Duluth and remembers the bounty of Minnesota's mines.

Most of my work around railroad cars was with ore cars on the ore docks. Mostly 75-ton jobs that ran late in World War II. They replaced the smaller 40- to 50-ton cars from the early days and the hundred-ton jobs had not been made yet.

I helped unload ore at the ore docks, though I rarely touched ore. We loosened ore so that it flowed out of the bottom doors of the cars for loading on the ore ships. This was big business in '43, '44, and '45. The war had the steel mills on the Great Lakes hungry for taconite from the mines around Lake Superior.

The taconite ore cars were improvements on the standard gravel cars that were used earlier for ore. The doors were less likely to jam. But that didn't mean the loads came out any easier. After all, taconite doesn't run as slick as sand or wheat, and a car takes a beating running down from the mines in 60-car lots.

Old-timers said it was lots better than the early days. They said the first cars were simple gondolas and were loaded and unloaded by crews with shovels. But that was before the big ore boats. Trains of ore went clear across Wisconsin and Illinois to mills in Indiana and Ohio. Small loads went by whaleback freighters on the lake. That, too, was loaded by hand.

I came to the job as a kid of 16 in the fall of '43. Already had two summers of loading gravel and grain. That's hard work, so I thought the ore docks would be easy. Especially since these cars were supposed to be the height of the engineering craft and were supposed to lose their loads like a baby on prune juice.

Well, nothing works out in practice the way it's supposed to in theory. In the old gravel cars there were a million ways that a pea-sized piece of gravel could jam up a door so that ten men with sledge hammers, pry bars, and blow torches couldn't budge it. Pound and curse, curse and pound, jam jacks into it, unload it by hand, and ram it with a locomotive. Some just refused to open their doors.

Now with the new 75-ton ore cars that was not the problem. Doors were usually slicker than Susie on Saturday night. But that didn't necessarily mean that the load would drop. No, it didn't mean that at all. We use to swear that those cars were magnetized and just refused to part with that iron. But it was usually load condition and material in the load that made our lives miserable. Little bit of aggregate, silt, and moisture and the thing could set like concrete. Same as can happen with gravel or coal.

So it was my job throughout the year to loosen that material. We had several sizes of iron bars with which to do it. A short stubby one for working from below, designed so you were just about certain of a face full of dust should the load cut loose. Then there was a long thin one that you poke down in the load from up on the car sides, just so you could definitely prove to your own satisfaction that it was inevitable that you get physically down in the car. At that juncture you had one other bar of medium length, with a widened edge like a bark-peeling spud. The design of this mechanical marvel just about guaranteed a laceration should the load gave way and should you fall upon the tool.

Now in the winter these delights were increased a hundredfold by the freezing of the loads. This is where steaming ore comes in. Then it was my job to "lance taconite," a maneuver not military nor medical. We had steam lances, devices to inject heat into the load. This was one of the main design features of the 75-ton Iron Range ore car. It had steam ports, little holes where you put the lance so as to loosen the ice in the load.

Ain't felt anything more nippy than that wind off the lake, whipping the ore dock with a whine like a jet engine, finding every loose patch in your pants, every little gap between glove and coat sleeve, and every tiny opening leading from your collar to the heart of your longjohns. Get the dust going at you like a brushfire when the wind whipped up through the bottom and you like to think you're getting sandblasted and readied for a new coat of paint. Then throw in some steam backwash, sometimes a scald, sometimes just warm and wet, and the dampness is driven by the wind right down to your skin only to set as frost between the layers of your clothes. I iced up so bad one day that my coats went board stiff and broke at the elbows like a cheap whiskey bottle on payday.

The cars snaked out of the Allouez Yard. They came our way through the interchanges of the various railroads serving the mines, mostly from the Mesabi Range, though I think we got some roundabout loads when there was trouble on the docks further east on the lake.

Lot of Great Northern ore cars. Quite a few from Northern Pacific and the Soo. Sometimes train after 60-car train of our local favorite, the Duluth, Missabe, and Iron Range Railway. A few times some Milwaukee Road, North Western, and other junk sent our way by the railroad war board. And if I remember correctly, we handled a lot of Canadian National and Duluth, Winnipeg, and Pacific loads until the Thunder Bay ore dock opened.

When those came we'd go, "Ho, ho, ho . . . a load from the North Pole." Guess those Maple Leafers were mining clear up to James Bay. Made us feel good to know that there was someone more stupid than an ore dock worker, though you couldn't be sure of that when you tallied up our wounds.

When it wasn't cold we were fighting. It was always something to bruise or bang you up. I was buried up to my neck in a jammed load. Saw more than one fellow slip and fall off the dock. It's quite a fall. Then there were the usual broken wrists, pinched off fingers, and crushed toes that you get around stubborn heavy equipment. It wasn't work for the dainty or faint of heart.

Go to modern power plants and look at how good those guys got it. No more doors and chutes. The cars got rotary couplers and can be turned upside down. You don't need a human being anywhere near the coal car. They work up in a control room with a computer. Talk to those fellows about steaming a load and they'll think you're nuts!

ORPHAN TRAINS

Railroads played a large part in many of America's social dramas. For the better part of a century, trains were the transitional vehicle in the lives of most people. Many a citizen and many a recently arrived immigrant used the train to begin a new life. Trains reunited families, brought home wounded soldiers, and returned bodies for burial. Almost every facet of train shipping and passenger travel enhanced the human condition.

Trains did not see widespread use in the transport of slaves, sparing railroads the bloody legacy of the African trading ships. Indeed, more than one runaway from the South's "peculiar institution" used a freight train pointed toward the North Star as transport to freedom. Even prisoners of war ranked train travel in crowded cattle cars superior to forced marches. Thus, rail strike violence aside, railroads had little legacy of suffering in the minds of most people.

There is a dwindling number of survivors who think otherwise. For them, train travel is associated with painful loss and rootlessness. Otto is now a great-grandfather living comfortably with three other generations in a farmhouse a half hour north of Burlington, Iowa. Listen in as he tells his family about their connection to the orphan trains.

You'll hear people talk about the "orphan train" as if there was only one. I guess for many there was only one that mattered, the one they were on. But there were lots of them, maybe seven to eight decades of them. Starting before the Civil War and going into the Depression.

The earliest orphan trains were used by New York City authorities to clear orphans out of tenements. Most were genuine orphans, parents killed in industrial accidents or by epidemics of disease. Some were simply separated from family by the chaos of the tenements, with parents away from the lodgings when the police made a raid on a building for other purposes. In the babble and confusion of immigrant tongues and with official indifference, children with two working parents could find themselves herded away. In a few cases, destitute and hopeless parents might even give their children up to an orphan train.

Many of these kids spoke no English. I didn't. The family who gave us their name and this farm told me they had no idea what language I spoke. They just set straightaway to teach me English. Some of the other older kids who came with me to Burlington thought we were Czech. Now I believe everyone in America should learn English, but I feel like something was ripped out of me by not even knowing what language I heard in my parents' laps. I'd love to sing you a song that I could say was sung to me by my mother in her native tongue. But I can't and it's gone.

Orphan trains ran out of the big eastern cities mostly. New York, of course, and Philadelphia, Boston, and Baltimore. Some of the smaller places back east too, mostly mill towns with bad conditions. The story was that our train came out of the Pennsylvania coal regions, though it could have been the hard coal area north of Philadelphia or the soft coal region around Pittsburgh. Probably will never know.

It's an ugly story for America. There were probably a half million of us over the years. That's a lot of children to uproot and shuttle around like cattle. Until right at the end, during the New Deal, when the social workers got in on it, there was no supervision of it at all. Just load the kids up and parade them around at different Midwest stops.

Makes you wonder why the railroads got involved in such a thing. Can you imagine today's airlines participating in a scheme to snatch up children in one place and transport them somewhere to be given away like kittens! Why there'd be an uproar! Unless the children were Cuban or Vietnamese, of course.

All the big railroads were in on it. Back east you had the New York Central leading the pack. Not far behind was the Pennsylvania Railroad. There was even orphan traffic on the Chesapeake & Ohio and the Baltimore & Ohio. All the big ones that came into Chicago. From there the kids were switched over to Midwest lines. As far as I can tell, Chicago & North Western was the leading orphan train line in the Midwest. But I've heard stories of orphan trains on the Illinois Central, the Rock Island, the Milwaukee Road, and the Burlington. Even of through-trains set up with Union Pacific and Southern Pacific to haul kids west to pick fruit.

That was at the root of a lot of the orphan train business, the need for farm labor. Guess that's why the railroads got involved. Kind of community relations. When the word of an orphan train would get out, farmers and their wives would make a day of it in town. Go shopping, pick up supplies, and go to the depot to look over the orphans. Maybe pick out a strong-looking boy.

This is how related children were often split up. Farmers would pick as if bidding on draft horses, while the well-off women in town would pick out the sweet little girls as future domestic help. You can imagine that there was many a tearful scene as brothers and sisters were split up at the depots. I knew one woman in Burlington who searched thirty years for her brother, only to discover that his adoptive family moved to a ranch in Colorado and that he died in a tank battle in North Africa in World War II.

Midwesterners had a populist etiquette about the selection process. If you had plucked one off the last orphan train, you let others have first crack at the new batch. Childless couples, especially the ones with those sad and lonely women, were given first pick of the litter. That usually worked out pretty well, since those women usually picked out cute little ones unfit for farm work. Then, if there were enough kids to go round, the man in such a family might get a second pick like in a sports draft. He'd be expected to go for height and muscle in the second round.

On the whole, these adoptive parents were decent people, if not loving and understanding. But there was nothing in place to check up on it. In fact, most of these situations were not formal adoptions. There wasn't any paperwork on most of them. Most of us don't even have birth certificates. It was a very informal process. There was no way to guard against child abuse or judge suitability of parents.

For most of us there was no open abuse, just strict rules and hard work. Pretty much what kids around here got from their own parents. But there was a dark side too. Kids that just disappeared. Kids that showed up in shallow graves. Grown-up orphans who never got right in their hearts or their minds and then spent adulthood in prison or the insane asylum.

I heard a story once about an orphan train that went to Des Moines. It was the depth of hard times and in the dead of winter. The orphans were unloaded, but only a few were picked out. People couldn't feed any extra mouths. The railroad wouldn't let the orphans back on the train, so a group of children wandered off in the cold. They found them frozen to death, huddled in a circle in an abandoned building. It was a huge embarrassment and it was hushed up.

So I consider myself lucky.

But I think about those who didn't make it or really suffered. I think about those split-up families, those lost siblings who died with holes in their hearts. There ought to be a monument to those children that we threw on the orphan train.

GHOST TRAIN

Railroad hauntings are a surprisingly common motif in train lore. Collectors of ghost lore in the Midwest have heard of dozens, if not hundreds, of phantoms of the rails. Usually such references are brief anecdotes, with sketchy details and little historical context.

Ghosts in the railroad setting often inhabit specific structures and sites. Hardly a rail tunnel was completed without loss of life. Many a trestle was the scene of a fatal accident. Throw in the train wrecks, depot fires, and roundhouse explosions and you have plenty of fodder for hauntings.

The most common form of railroad haunting is the lone sentinel. A long dead brakeman still trying to prevent a derailment. An engineer who told the crew to jump while he stayed on the engine, trying to stop it up to the last minute. A carman's spirit wandering an abandoned yard. Or an apparition of a gandy dancer still moving spritely among stacks of ties and rails.

Perhaps the rarest form of railroad haunting is the complete ghost train. This form usually involves phantom equipment and crew, and occasionally passengers. Or it can be an empty train, like the Lost Dutchman of the sea.

Consideration of such matters is a very specialized pursuit. There is little overlap among the communities of the rail fans and students of the paranormal. Ike is the only one I found. He was kind enough to share his research. Let's join him in a bar in Galesburg, Illinois.

Railroad ghosts? Dime a dozen! At least stories. Real sightings, witnesses, and facts to back it up, well, that's a different matter. Like other ghost tales, you have to sift through the things seen by drunks and hysterics and weed out the practical jokes and the hoaxes. But, then you get down to a core of more intriguing stuff.

Nearly every big yard or major station had a ghost story. Mostly they're forgotten, but I try to collect them. It's the phantom trains that are a bit more elusive. The most common form is sound, things like engine noise, bells, and whistles where trains don't run anymore. But some are seen and a few in great detail.

One noted in paranormal circles was an old Milwaukee Road way freight on the Mineral Point line in Wisconsin. That was a natural since it was in an area thick with ghosts. It was a simple ghost train, with one engine, two boxcars, and a caboose. It was seen after abandonment of the line and even after the tracks were gone.

Those kinds of phantom trains seem to have a basis. There's another on the old Chicago & North Western narrow gauge line into Fennimore, Wisconsin. I'm investigating such sightings on the Omaha and another on the Fort Dodge.

The premier ghost train is a Burlington passenger train. A Denver Zephyr to be precise. Very distinctive because of the shovelnose stainless steel power car. You have to know a bit of rail history to even know what that is. One fellow thought he saw a UFO following railroad tracks. He didn't believe a train, especially one from the 1930s, could look like that. So I showed him the pictures.

The design marked this specific ghost train as particular to a very narrow time frame: 1934 to 1939. Those were the years of shovelnose power units on the Denver Zephyr. After that they still used stainless steel sheathed engines, but of different design. It is a very specific phenomenon, with a precise configuration of cars.

What does it mean? That's what I'm still trying to figure out. I haven't uncovered any big tragedy that connects to that train in that era. You'd think for a phenomenon like that, the whole thing and everybody on it must have been destroyed. But I've yet to find evidence of mass destruction. Such a thing would be hard to cover up, unless the government was involved. It was in that time just before World War II, the time of Amelia Earhart, preparations for the Manhattan Project, and research for a variety of secret weapons. So, you never know.

But it could have simpler explanations than that. Spirit manifestations are connected to energy in nature in many ways. Our subconscious is tuned in to that energy even if our minds are not. It's a two-way street. It could be the spirit energy of those on that train in that time, a distillation of a moment so powerful that it is a moment they can repeat again and again. Or it could be the subconscious desires of the living.

Think about it. What frame of reference generates more longing and nostalgia than the passenger trains of the golden age of railroading? Might not that energy summon up these trains of the past? Might not there be spirits in that time eager to reveal themselves to those open to the experience?

On a paranormal level, it could be many things. It could be a window into time, a tear in what we see as immutable physics. Or, it could be rail fans of the future who have mastered time and can bring back classic trains for excursions in different periods. Maybe it's a projection or image sent interdimensionally as a message.

All I know is when I see it there's a quality to it that is very warm and human. It's always at night in the winter months. The passengers look out the windows or converse among themselves. There is joy on their faces. This train is aglow on the inside and outside it gleams in starlight. It is a magic vessel for dreams coursing through the night.

What to make of such a thing? One part of me wants to figure it out, the other part reveres the mystery. One part of me wants proof that something paranormal is really happening, the other part secretly hopes that the ghost train will stop and allow me to board.

LITTLE BOY'S EYES

Rail yarns can sometimes get hung up on terminology and historic background. Rail buffs are an exacting lot, and rail employees and retirees sometimes have the aloofness of a fraternity. It is not always easy to be a casual observer of trains and their environments.

Yet press the railworkers, expert modelers, or affluent rail fans, and nine times out of ten you'll extract a confession that the passion all began with simple pleasures. Ask them to go back in their memory to find their first consciousness of trains. Almost always the story is one of childhood joy.

That's Martin's message. His modest Green Bay home has no collectible railroad heralds or antique caboose lights. This youngish-looking grandfather and street department worker has passed on the toy trains of his boyhood to his children and grandchildren. He knows what trains are all about for the great majority of Americans.

Watching the trains started naturally enough for me. Dad and all his brothers worked at the yard. That would be the Green Bay and Western yard, the center of my early universe. Whole bunches of cousins took me down there young, probably three or four years old.

They let me in on the last of the steam era. Boy, did I love to watch those things, smoke and steam and sounds to catch the young eye. But I'd watch engines and trains if they were powered by hamsters on treadmills.

The family was all over the yard map, as they liked to say. Some were switching, some fixed cars, Uncle Roy ran the roundhouse, and Dad was a hostler until that went by the wayside. After that I think he was something called an engine watchman. I was proud of him as could be.

A hostler brings the engine in from the storage track and moves it over to the cinder pit. There they "knock" the fire, which means they clean it. If they need to turn around quick, there's just a quick inspection, oiling and cleaning. If in for major repairs, the engine is moved on the maintenance track and cooled.

Dad talked about three classes of repairs. I think it was classes A, B, and C. Class C was two to ten days. Class B was eleven to thirty days. And class A was over thirty days. Heavier stuff might go either to the Milwaukee shops or the North Western shops.

Green Bay and Western did not stand on ceremony. Dad would some-times help out on short maintenance like boiler washing, which was basically a half day of flushing. There was other light stuff of lubrication service that he would do when it was slow. On a small railroad like that, Uncle Roy could get away with bringing the kids in to watch.

We'd watch the whole process and when it was done the engine would go from a service class to a call class on the board. If the round-house was busy the engine went back to the storage track. If they needed it immediately it made the rounds of the sand house, water tower, and coal chute.

Other days we watched the switching and making up of trains. Most fun was watching the little diesels that first got in for the local jobs. Sometimes a dozen kids might follow a load of lumber or cement down the sidings to customers. We'd run and laugh the whole way. Except for us shortlegs, we mostly kept up.

We did not confine our attentions to the Green Bay and Western. When we got older we had the run of the whole town and could watch crossings and interchanges. Who all did we have, Milwaukee Road, Chicago & North Western, and Soo Line? Lots of action and lots of fun. No shortage of crews that loved to show off for kids. The bigwigs would have been surprised by how many engine rides we managed to take. I'll tell you, the hayrides out at Granddad's Kewaunee County farm were nice but they just didn't compare to an engine cab.

When my turn came they weren't hiring and were unraveling like a cheap sweater. So I didn't get to railroad. Maybe just as well, wouldn't want to put my family through the ups and downs. For a while it looked like Green Bay might not have rail service. But there are new guys in town.

I don't know much about these companies. Don't know anyone who works for them. But I'll tell you something, it all comes back when I take my little grandson down by the tracks. Just to see him clap his hands in delight. Just to watch the wonder in his eyes. What more can you ask of a railroad?

IMMIGRANT TRAIN

Railroad tales are not always personal accounts of work or travel. Sometimes they are auxiliary to other human dramas and find their way into broader community lore. Often these echoes of life past will reveal historical tidbits and share humor of a prior day. A few drip with the poignancy of tragedy in hard times.

Much of the narrative of the Great Middle of America is derived from the rigorous pioneer experiences of immigrants. The ethnic groups in such stories are varied, but it is perhaps the Scandinavians who most captured the popular imagination. Earlier settlers on the prairies and in the North Woods were hardened generation by generation as they fought, cut, and tilled their way across the Appalachians, Ohio, and Indiana. Norwegian, Swedes, and their Finnish neighbors often found themselves in a strange log hut or sod dugout within weeks of landing in eastern ports.

Hunger, disease, starvation, and madness claimed some before their first year was out. Many with such roots joke to themselves that their early ancestors' existence was so hard that Lutheran pulpits to this day remain dour and pessimistic. This self-deprecating glumness was reinforced all the more among these peoples when the immigrants did not make it to their destination.

Alfred, a retired pastor in Mountain Lake, Minnesota, knows of such a tale from several angles. It is all the proof one needs that a forgotten tragedy can reverberate just as long as a major historical event.

The Omaha Line was the railroad in those early days. Of course, I mean the early part of the twentieth century. Back in a time when our farmland was still being advertised in the newspapers of Oslo, Norway. An age when bewildered-looking Norwegians got off trains and contemplated how they might apply fishing and shipbuilding skills to the tasks of winter wheat and dairy cows.

It was not uncommon for the railroad to bring in a car or two of immigrant families. Sometimes it would be a party of married men traveling alone, scouting for land, and hoping to bring families later. Many became longtime citizens of the area and everyone recognizes the family names.

In the spring of 1916, a tragedy struck. It was that time of year when we are full of hope and dreams, waiting for that green renewal. The equinox marks the return of the warm sun, and Easter, for the faithful, marks the ascension from winter's tomb. It was a good time for prudent immigrants to look at land and attempt to get established with a small crop and a warm shelter.

A car of immigrants sat in a combination train at the depot that spring. It was a short train with the immigrants' car just in front of a wooden caboose and behind a mail and baggage car. Some say that a few empty ice cars were just behind the engine's tender. They did not show up in the local newspaper account. But perhaps other cars were overlooked.

Omaha Freight Number 20 rolled into Mountain Lake a bit too fast to see that the switch would put them down the track where the immigrant train was sitting. The collision was massive and completely collapsed the caboose and pushed it into the immigrants' car. The wood cars splintered and pinned the passengers in the train.

Under some circumstances that would have been the extent of the damage. Some might have died of injuries anyway. But the next development generated the grimmest of fatalities. The caboose woodstove, trapped in wreckage, leaked its hot embers into the kindling pile that was sitting on the tracks. The fire spread into the immigrants' car and only a few were pulled to safety.

Based on church records, it seems that at least four perished in that fire. Their charred remains were found together at the collision end of the car. They were buried in our churchyard under the assumption that they were related, possibly a father and his sons. Their baggage revealed nothing about them other than their Norwegian origins. Their personal documents must have burned up with them.

Surely, the locals thought, someone will come looking for them or telegraph the railroad. But nothing happened that spring, summer, or fall. By winter people concluded that the four immigrants left no survivors. Residents bemoaned the tragedy and speculated about the intent and destination of the immigrants.

In the meantime a secondary impact of the tragedy manifested itself. The engineer of Freight Number 20 grew morose and eventually developed full blown depression. He could not forgive himself the error of judgment. He lost his job and took to drink, and his family fell upon the charity of the church. He, too, came to lie in the churchyard.

Mountain Lake thought that closed the book on the matter. Not quite. Two years after the accident another train brought a young girl of about ten years to Mountain Lake. Pinned to her overcoat was a note in English that said her father and three brothers had gone ahead to Mountain Lake. The note also reported on the death of the mother during an influenza outbreak.

The engineer's family took that girl in, raised her, and helped her decorate those four immigrant graves in the churchyard. She married into that family and made that German clan into a thoroughly Norwegian bunch. The descendants still remember her holidays, her recipes, and her songs. Five generations since know of the immigrant train.

RAILROAD DIGS

Before the advent of the great half-continent runs, like Broadway Limited and Empire Builder, rail travel was more akin to stage travel, with complicated connections and many overnight stops. Even at the height of twentieth-century rail travel, a transcontinental trip might require, or at least merit, a layover in Chicago, St. Louis, or Memphis. Elsewhere, in the backwaters and on the local runs, sleeping accommodations were never far from the thought of the long distance traveler.

This was all part of the lifestyle for traveling salesmen and other wandering itinerants. For the immigrant or farmer seeking new land it was part of a one-time adventure, and spartan quarters did not faze those hearty souls. Captains of industry dealt with their needs by building private cars. The more economy minded might try to catch forty winks in a coach or splurge on a sleeper for part of a long trip and then wander the streets of the layover town.

Recreational travel for the masses was one outgrowth of the continent-wide web of tracks and trains. Suddenly, ordinary people could travel to just about anywhere in the country. A market grew for honeymoon and family outing travel. With it came the need for affordable and reliable lodging.

This auxiliary service sector, like the railroads themselves, expanded by fits and starts. It evolved considerably through the years and few living could claim to know the stages personally. Benjamin, a businessman in Mullion, Illinois, comes close.

Grandmother Barker had me a seasoned traveler before I was ten. What an independent old gal, traveling the country with a boy. Or as she put it, "a strong boy to handle the baggage and a hardwood cane to ward off the villains." She kept emphasizing that she needed me to carry the bags, but I knew before I was six that she was really devoted to broadening my horizons.

She was quite an adventurer, willing to go anywhere and with eyes wide with discovery right up to, and including, her last breath at 81. She was widowed in her middle forties and left comfortable with income-producing properties. Her children married well and she had few cares. So in those middle and later years she gave herself up to her passion to see new sights and experience new things.

Her curiosity was a direct hands-on thing. She didn't want to watch from afar. So it was from her I gained my knowledge of the four basic classes of railroad accommodations. As she put it, there was the bottom tier of dives and flops. Then you had your rooming houses, with a range of cleanliness and family suitability. In the vacation areas you had your lodges. In the cities were the downtown station hotels.

In the bigger cities you also might have a downtown grand hotel in proximity to a major rail station. Grandmother Barker felt they were over-priced and, as she said, "full of stuffy and uninteresting people." She'd rather dance a jig with people fresh from Ireland or trade recipes with an Italian cook in a sweaty kitchen reeking of garlic.

Believe me, she did not avoid the seamy spots. I saw her drink whiskey with drunken cowboys in Sheridan, Wyoming. I remember her laugh on our first overnight on the train trip in Mexico. She was stubborn enough in the face of full hotels to insist that the local bordello might have a room. A good-humored madam capitulated and we spent two nights. Grand-mother listened to the girls' hard luck stories and paid off the debt of one and bought her a bus ticket back to the family village. I had an interesting time being petted by the señoritas, and they told me to come back at age eighteen. Which I did.

She also liked the scenic places. Few remember how the railroads really opened up the American consciousness to our natural treasures. I know, you could say that it started the problem of loving the places to death. But I think the environment was much better off with a few train cars of visitors arriving near a national park than with the need for parking lots and access roads for thousands of automobiles a day.

I really enjoyed the lodges in the natural areas and resorts. In my boy-hood you could still book your package through the railroad. This meant rail travel, lodging, connections out to the scenic areas, and guided services all in one deal. Your connections might be a bus, a farm truck, a ferry, a rowboat, or a pack mule. We traveled the Milwaukee Road with a side package to Yellowstone. We took the Chicago & North Western to a con-nection to the Big Horn Mountains. We rode the Great Northern to Glacier National Park. Was it the Soo Line that got us up close to Mackinac Island? Memories play tricks. But I'm pretty sure it was the Seaboard Coast Line that got us down to the Everglades. All with clean lodges wait-ing for us and friendly staff who couldn't do enough for you. None of that "you want fries with that" attitude.

The best of the best had to be the Great Northern set up at Glacier National Park. The rail scenery doesn't get much better than that. If I'm not mistaken, the lodge there was railroad owned and run like a cross between a dude ranch and a fine dining car. Food, activities, grizzled cowpokes strumming guitars at campfires—they had it all. Grandmother Barker even had it arranged so that when we arrived, an outfit of chaps, blue jeans, western shirt, cowboy hat, and holstered toy pistols was waiting in the room on my made-up daybed. I tell you, one little boy sure slept happy.

But it wasn't all about big trips. Some of the best trips were closer to home. There was a place where we'd go in summer on the Milwaukee Road to Tomahawk, Wisconsin. Beautiful spot to fish off the lodge dock, just like a Leinenkugel ad. Once we even did a rail excursion to a church camp. I think it was Green Lake, Wisconsin. Grandmother had a lady friend who had an inn down in the southern Illinois coal hills that we'd take the Illinois Central to, and the depot clerk would drive us ten miles up a dirt road for a one dollar tip.

She taught me the ins and outs of the boardinghouses. Which ones had warmth to them, people sharing not only a bathroom but friendly conversation on a dark porch on a hot summer night. And which ones smelled desperate with the sweat of wife beaters. The good boarding-houses are still my favorite place to stay when I can find them.

The downtown hotels have taken a beating. The decline of rail travel sealed the fate of many. Others dropped several notches into dive and flop categories. Some of them are overrun with drug addicts, mentally ill, and assorted down-and-outers. The other problem is that they're often in the worst part of a town.

When I do my middle-class rail bumming I still like to check out the little town dives and flops. I'm kind of an upscale hobo with a credit card and a cellular phone. With a game leg I can't hop a freight anymore like I did in my college summers. But occasionally I'll sweet-talk a crew into a ride. It was sure easier when there were cabooses. More and more I'm driving the Oldsmobile out to the small rail towns.

Sometimes I'm stuck with a cheap motel some distance from the yards. But if you poke around and get to know the crews you'll sometimes luck into a real gem. Find a place where railroaders with families elsewhere take rooms by the week or month. One of my favorites used to be in Portage, Wisconsin. A place called the Party House, a bar next to the yard with about six rooms upstairs. Not a loud joint from the bar but you'll get plenty vibration from the train action.

These places and their history are as much a part of the railroad scene as the rolling stock. Bankruptcies and mergers take the toll, short lines come and go, and the towns themselves go from golden age to decay to renewal. But the rail lodgings hang on and you can get the flavor of the past in them. Maybe even more importantly, you can reconnect with that long gone person who first got you out and about and put travel in your blood. I know I feel close to Grandmother Barker in those rooms.

VALLEY CHARACTERS

Celebrity encounters during train rides are generally thought of in terms of the passenger trains that carried Hollywood stars, baseball players, and prize-fighters in the days before air travel. Travelers of genuine notoriety sometimes made their ways across America in private cars or other accommodations segregated from ordinary passengers. A passenger's claim to a brush with fame was often based solely on reports from a porter or conductor that a luminary was elsewhere on the train.

Yet, the genuine democratic heroes of the American public left lasting impressions based upon their ability to be both accessible and sociable in the confines of railroad coaches. This tradition seemed to flow from the tours of acclaimed Union Army generals to the encampments of the Grand Army of the Republic. It was further reinforced by the rail travels of populists and social reformers like William Jennings Bryan, Eugene Debs, Mother Jones, and John L. Lewis. Even our entertainers from Mark Twain to Will Rogers to the big bands of the 1940s reinforced myths of their mastery of the common touch with pleasantries bestowed on fellow rail travelers.

Local train runs, of course, also had their celebrity passengers. Access to the well known was all the more comfortable when it fit within the pattern of a regular commute or routine errand trip to a nearby town. Such is the stuff of Russell's memories. The silver-haired Spring Green, Wisconsin, resident sits in the General Store Cafe and tells the tale of a unique area with a few unique travelers.

Everybody wants to know about Derleth and Wright. Or Old Augie and His Royal Highass, as Pop used to call August Derleth and Frank Lloyd Wright. Both were genuine characters molded by the Wisconsin River valley. Both shifted like sandbars, could be cold as a rocky bluff and unpredictable as a spring flood. But they weren't the only ones. This area has drawn such characters since the French discovered the Indians' portage.

The coming of the trains put these fellows—well, mostly fellows— out where the public could rub elbows with them. And, like Derleth and Wright, they weren't always too sociable. I think it was the color they added to a train ride that stuck in the tales told here in the valley.

Far as I know, the original has to be Captain James Black. He was supposed to be an ancient Black Hawk War veteran who made a virtual career of riding the first trains in the valley. Supposedly the conductors let him ride free, a precedent that haunted subsequent crews trying to corral fares out of celebrities.

Captain Black had a bad limp which he attributed to a musket ball put in his leg by none other than old Black Hawk himself. It was said that Captain Black could hold the attention of an entire coach with his hoarse whispered accounts of the battles at Pecatonica, Wisconsin Heights, and Bad Axe. He would talk about conversations he had with Abraham Lincoln and Jefferson Davis in their soldiering days. It was customary for passengers to take up a collection for Captain Black, though it was commonly acknowledged that the proceeds went for the purchase of whiskey.

In a side note, it should be mentioned that Captain Black claimed to be one of the original investors in the Milwaukee and Waukesha Railway. He said he helped survey the valley route that had Prairie du Chien as its objective. Then he supposedly lost everything in one of those bank panics that would hit every few years in those times. Guess he just disappeared eventually, but way before my time.

Then there was Old Buck, a Civil War veteran who made it practically up to my day. Pop knew him well. You might say that Old Buck was Captain Black's understudy and worked the same game. But it was said that the two disabled veterans did not get along during their decades of overlap. Guess they didn't like to work the same crowd.

Pop said the old-timers in his day insisted that Captain Black and Old Buck never got on the same train. It went so far as to where one would get off if he saw the other boarding. By Pop's boyhood, Old Buck had the train all to himself. Valley boys were regaled with accounts of Gettysburg and other such turning points in history. As with Captain Black, no one knew if the accounts were exaggerated or had any factual basis at all. And, as with Captain Black, there was the tradition of riding the train without paying.

Those were some of the famed passengers in the early days, at least the ones that I can be sure were based on actual, if not altogether truthful, people. But how can you leave out the passengers of legend? The valley has more than its share of larger-than-life characters that seem to assert themselves into accounts in wildly different time periods. Things like the famed boatman River Rat Fred straightening a flood-ravaged section of rails and ties like you might snap straight a tablecloth or bedsheet. Tales of a frontier madam called Iron Lena entertaining in a private car. Myths involving phantom train appearances by Whiskey Jack or dozens of valley ghosts.

That's the stuff that sets the table for train encounters with Derleth and Wright. There are still quite a few valley people living who sat in coaches with both of those strange fellows. Watching them on the trains was a form of entertainment in those days. But it was definitely two different types of shows.

Both were abrasive men, full of themselves. But Derleth had the more common touch. If he felt that the valley was peopled by idiots, he at least fondly regarded them as "his" idiots. Wright, on the other hand, was thoroughly imperial in his approach to the local peasants, ignoring bills from tradesmen and vendors as if their services were due him as feudal rent.

One Milwaukee Road conductor who knew both men said he got to like Derleth but could never stand to be in the same coach as Wright. He confessed that he liked Derleth's regional literature despite detecting himself in a story as a hick from the sticks. Any Derleth quirks were just chalked up to those bohemian behaviors that we allowed artists in the days before televangelists ran politics. He said if Derleth was arrogant, it was the good-natured exuberant ego of a small town high school football coach with a long winning streak.

Wright, on the other hand, was described as the Antichrist. The great architect of leaky-roof buildings could apparently charm a room of wide-eyed students but had no use for anyone employed by a railroad. Wright treated all of them like his personal servants and seemed to take any difficulty in travel as a personal affront. Wright berated clerks, chastised baggage handlers, neglected to tip porters, insulted conductors, and wrote provocative notes to engineers. He was known and disliked by workers on all the railroads that served Madison.

But the ones that outright hated Wright were on the Milwaukee Road. The conductor told me that once Wright had him deliver a snotty note to an engineer and the engineer turned red faced when he read it. The engineer said he'd work on an answer and stuffed the note down in the rear end of his overalls, worked it around, pulled it out, wiped it in the corner where the fireman sometimes emptied his bladder, worked up a mountain of mucus thickened by tobacco juice to inscribe on the note, and folded the whole assembly into a dispatch envelope. "Here's my reply," said the engineer.

It was this conductor who had the famed running battle with Wright to collect a fare. Derleth didn't always pay either, but it was thought to be forgetfulness and preoccupation with the joys of the train ride. Wright had an attitude that his presence was payment.

Wright would board the train with theatrical flourishes, swinging that silly cape of his like a bullfighter. Then he would glare at people in the aisles if they were between him and his seat. Finally, he would sit with his arms folded, a haughty look on his face that said to all the world: "Try and make me pay or try and put me off the train."

The conductor did not think Wright was worth the effort of that type of confrontation. But he couldn't let it go entirely. So he would ask Wright for the ticket in the tone one might use on an incorrigible deadbeat or a mental defective. "Oh, you've probably lost the ticket again," he'd say. "That's fine, the men losing their farms and the widows and orphans will make up for it."

The conductor counted it a good day when he could see the telltale hint of anger bulging Wright's collar. Wright tried hard not to register emotion about such things and would counter with unreasonable demands, calling for such things as the latest copy of a Chicago newspaper or a cup of tea. The conductor's day wasn't complete until he had arranged for Wright's luggage to be delivered to a platform location where mongrel dogs did their business.

Other differences between Wright and Derleth? Plenty of them. But those of us who remember valley passenger service know that Wright didn't like those train rides. Derleth, heck, what he was about came from those train rides.

RAILROAD CANTEEN

Wartime railroad stories left a deep impression on the World War II generation. Many Midwest families treasure stories about tearful farewells on station platforms, with more than a few of these tales representing the last time a loved one was seen. Rail travel in wartime was often a grim business, with trains crowded to the seams with reluctant passengers herded off to distant assignments.

Still, many positive memories came out of those times. For some, the troop train was the first taste of freedom after basic training and was the site of all the hijinks that young men can devise after weeks of strict discipline. For others, the train was the instrument of reunion.

Not that sad partings, jostling travels, and joyful returns were the only stories of those times. There were also meetings. Never before had so many young adults from different parts of the United States been able to meet members of the opposite sex outside of their own neighborhoods and ethnic groups.

U.S.O. clubs were the most notable meeting spots in those troubled years, with many in or near major railroad stations. In the major cities, these clubs were often the hottest nightspots in town. In New York the big bands would swing for the dancing pleasure of large crowds. In Hollywood, the movie starlets brought glitter into seas of khaki.

Midwest rail centers could seldom compete on the celebrity level, often lacking a U.S.O. unless the town had a military installation nearby. But many heartland rail depots, stations, and whistle-stops had "canteens." A rail station canteen was a place where soldiers, sailors, and marines could relax, grab a sandwich, and otherwise engage in diversions.

Elsie, a widow with an old hillside house overlooking the Mississippi in Dubuque, Iowa, remembers the canteens. Put on some Andrews Sisters music, pull up a chair, and go back to the 1940s.

Railroad canteens were usually considered part of the railroad business, though we received precious little support from them. The labor was almost entirely volunteer, the majority being railroad wives or daughters. Some were motivated by wartime patriotism, others by concern for the well-being of young men away from home, and others by the small town hope that behavior problems could be confined to a limited area.

My attitude was one of helping the war effort. I was the young wife of an older Burlington Route engineer. He was a World War I veteran and the old fool went again in World War II when he didn't have to. He was in the railroad battalions in Europe and was disabled from frostbite.

So after he went back in the army in the summer of 1942, I found myself looking for things to do. I was considered too small for most defense work. My sister was also a railroad wife in Omaha and she told me about a railroad clerking job there with the Union Pacific. It sounded like an adventure to me, so off I went. Made quite an impression when I arrived with my French flowered hat, white gloves, and fox wrap. They were expecting a big-boned farm girl who could lift packages and mailbags. They put me in an office with a typewriter and eventually I learned how to use it.

So my clerk days were not ones of adventure. I barely knew what was happening on the railroad. I soon tired of playing cards with my sister in the evening. I just had to find something else to keep me busy. That's when I found out about the canteen.

It was just the thing for me. I had a fair voice in my day and a bit of skill with the piano. I had the social grace expected of a pastor's child and could serve tea with the best of the seminary faculty wives. Little did I know that many of the soldiers expected me to act like a saloon girl, not a lady weaned on theological discussions at the dinner table.

Most of the soldiers were well behaved, they were just a little rough hewn. And, oh so young. Many younger than I at my innocent twenty-five. Not at all like the clergy and professors of religion that made up the circle of males in my world. Even my railroading husband was a refined man and deacon in his church.

The canteen was in Omaha's Union Station. That was as fine a passenger facility as one could find in the Corn Belt. Not as palatial as New York or Chicago, mind you, but a clean and dignified terminal that fit

Nebraskan sensibilities. It was quite a step up from my cell in the freight offices. It was a fine location for a canteen.

World War II veterans have many memories of the canteens, especially in the Midwest. I hear from Boston Irish who remember pheasant sandwiches in South Dakota at the Milwaukee Road canteen. An Italian man from Philadelphia told me of a Christmas Eve spent in the canteen in North Platte, another Union Pacific stop. The connecting points on the Illinois Central, Sante Fe, and Chicago North Western all had their good points and good memories.

Many of those memories were romantic memories. You have no idea how many midwestern women met their future husbands in those canteens, how many sweethearts fought their way to platforms just for a glimpse of a boyfriend coming through from training on one coast and bound for invasion armadas on the opposite coast, and how many new brides went there in hope of a brief honeymoon.

This last group became my specialty during my canteen days. I would meet these girls, most younger than I, and listen to their stories. It was familiar territory for those who lived in those times. A quick justice of the peace wedding moments before the groom's departure for training, followed by his unscheduled transfer to another base, and wrapped up with short notice orders to coastal embarcation ports.

These brides had detective skills worthy of the most cunning German spies. They knew if a soldier from Fort So-and-So left the East Coast on the New York Central or the Baltimore & Ohio and was bound for San Francisco, then he would pass through Omaha. Sometimes they would show me telegrams from other war brides in crude codes telling when a certain military unit passed through Cleveland, Chicago, or Louisville.

My soft heart put me at the disposal of these newlyweds. Any skills in the arts of deception and manipulation that I may have developed in the course of my life are traceable to my role as canteen cupid. I would procure short-term lodging for the couples in train crew hotels. I would type up rail employee travel passes that allowed brides to evade wartime travel restrictions. With gratuities to Union Pacific porters, stewards, and chefs, I could arrange rarities of fine linens, champagne, anniversary cakes, and room service meals.

Those brides were "my girls." They still are. We have a reunion every few years. Most are now widows like me. Some live on Montana ranches, some in retirement communities in Florida, some in exclusive suburbs, and one even with her grandchildren in a commune in the Ozarks.

The brides were far from the only romance centered around the canteen. It sometimes happened that a fifteen-minute wait for a train would bring about a deep encounter that was followed by three or four years of correspondence. Read those letters and you will see that many of the men survived on that love and hope.

On occasion we would see a romance with the roles reversed. I was matron of honor for an army nurse who married a passenger train conductor. Oh my, I remember how happy they were. I also remember the pain my heart felt when I learned that she went down with a troop ship in the South Pacific.

We all seemed so alive in that time, though we knew that it could end so quickly and tragically. As a woman alone in those years, I was not immune from the intense emotions that went with the wartime way of life. There were innocent encounters that left many bittersweet memories about what might have been.

My main work in the canteen put me in close quarters with many rowdy soldiers and sailors. As I would sing and play the piano I was often at the center of an exuberant party with all manner of strange men trying to kiss me and ask me out on dates. But those were not my types of men.

Where I felt the naughty pleasures of flirtation were in the more serious cultural activities we offered. I managed our art supplies and servicemen's art exhibits. I also helped in the canteen's reading room, reshelving books and stocking newspapers from around the country. It was these canteen activities that put me in company of the more thoughtful types. It was there that I met former teachers, journalists, and seminary students.

My heart was touched a time or two, though my modesty remained intact. It was a place where I learned much about life. In the canteen I gained the confidence to go back to college. In the canteen I learned that you can't let life pass you by.

SHIP JUMPER, TRAIN HOPPER

Heartland rail stories are fertile territory for tie-ins with other transportation modes. Containerized freight piggyback trailers, barges, and ships all have their rail links in our section of the country. Ship traffic is particularly rail dependent for dockside delivery of agricultural commodities and raw materials.

Great Lakes shipping started with a strange relationship to railroads. The first locomotives and rolling stock in the area delivered by ship to Chicago. The early, pre–St. Lawrence Seaway days saw the equation reversed from today: ships delivered commodities to the railheads for transport to the coasts. Train ferries even saved time by hauling cars across narrow points in the lakes.

Rail lore in the region gets a maritime flavor from such influences. Older stories still tell us of boxcars of salt fish headed west, of logs rafted to bays and loaded on flatcars, and of patrol boats and submarines built in Great Lakes ports making "maiden voyages" on trains bound for saltwater naval bases.

Great Lakes rail buffs can readily find tales about events and characters who mesh the worlds of trains and ships. Dockworkers, longshoremen, and port warehousemen are particularly good sources. Newt wouldn't consent to a meeting in his Duluth, Minnesota, boardinghouse, so we met east of the St. Louis River at a colorful tavern, the Anchor Bar and Grill in Superior, Wisconsin.

Look at those faces! There's a nip in the air, the feel of early winter closing in on the lakes. You can see it in the looks of the merchant seamen. They want to be clear of Lake Superior before it turns ugly. Close of the shipping season always brings that feel. Things have to be rushed before we settle in for the long nap.

Most railroaders don't understand the maritime schedule. Most are year-round plodders by nature. They seldom think about watching the sky or looking to the harbor signals. Just not in their genes. Only met one fellow who could move in both worlds, trains and ships, and he was a special case. He was always just one step ahead of trouble.

I'll call him Eric for the sake of a name. He's pretty much done it all around ships, docks, and railroads in a way that will tickle your fancy. His father was an American seaman from Minnesota who spent just enough dallying time in Norway to give Eric his start. So he grew up in a railroading family in Norway, in his grandfather's house.

In Norway he apprenticed as a brakeman on a switching crew in a major port. Before that he was a laborer on the docks. But he was pulled by the sea too, having sailor and fisherman blood in his veins. First it pulled him to ride the ferries to Europe. Then he pestered captains of small fishing boats to allow him aboard as an unpaid helper. That in turn led to his taking leave from his switching job in port and signing on with the big factory fishing ships that scour the North Atlantic. Finally he finagled a seaman's union card and made the transition to mercantile shipping.

Eric's introduction to the Great Lakes came through the grain trade after the St. Lawrence Seaway opened. He soon came to view Duluth and Superior as a second home. The yearning to see more of America overcame him and after a few trips he jumped ship. Now in most situations this would have been the end of the story. In many ports such a fellow would have fallen into a life of crime among the lowlifes, almost certain arrest, and eventual deportation.

But up north here, we value these virile Scandinavians. They remind us of our fabled Viking ancestors. Eric was given many a meal and warm place to sleep courtesy of railroaders, boatmen, and dockworkers here in the twin ports. We also taught him the ropes for things here in America.

How to hop freights, what routes to use, and how to find work on track crews and docks.

He was a good pupil. Not only did he cross America several times by train, but he became fluent in English and developed quite a following among the ladies. It wasn't too long before he could pass for American and gain acceptance in any rail yard, wharf district, or workingman's bar. He had a smile like the Northern Lights, a chin as strong as an anvil, and arms as stout as a lake schooner mast. In other words, a man's man.

It was said that even the most ornery of Great Northern rail tramps were gentled by his presence on a train or in a hobo jungle by the yard. He had a fondness for hopping the GN freights out to the Pacific. He loved the Rockies and the train trips through the high passes. The old GN railroad bulls, or private police, said that theft and vandalism always declined when Eric was riding the rails.

Now he could have made a decent career out of any one of a dozen occupations that he made the rounds of. He was good at them all. Many an employer saw fit to provide him with birth certificate, social security card, driver's license, and passport lest questions of his identity and citizenship speed his departure.

But he just had those darn itchy feet. There was always something else to do on the lakes or the railroads. Always something else to see or experience. One time it might be following the taconite from mine to train to dock to steel mill. Another time it might be hopping a sleepy way freight to a Lake Superior town, hitchhiking to a nearby Chippewa reservation, and rising early to help with whitefish nets.

Summers often found him on section crews working up travel money. He said he was personally acquainted with every tie in northern Wisconsin, northern Minnesota, Upper Peninsula, Michigan, and the main lines of North Dakota. No matter it be Milwaukee Road, Soo Line, Chicago & North Western, or Great Northern and its Burlington Northern offspring.

Could he ever handle ties. One of a few who could manhandle a switch tie. That's the thing, he could do any job well but was always talking about the next one. Everybody he ever worked with found him real entertaining. If a crew was replacing ties he told them stories of the high seas. If he was helping set nets he talked about cleaning up Milwaukee Road derailments. If he was smoking a pipe with a Soo conductor he'd talk about fishing boat breakfasts of lake trout. If he was working a grain hold he'd regale his coworkers with tales of bare-knuckled fights up at the iron mines.

It gave men a look at life over the horizon, down the line, and on the big blue. That's why they liked him. He was a free spirit. He lived like many of us dreamed. It was said that he had Finnish girlfriends in Marquette,

Escanaba, Hurley, Ashland, Superior, and Grand Portage and a saucy Frenchie in Thunder Bay. That classed him with the immortals.

Where did he go? Some say he was on false papers on the Edmund Fitzgerald. Some say he made his identity transition complete and became an engineer on the BN. Those who knew him best say he just moved on. One got postcards of banana boats and those Central American railroads. Who knows?

FIFTY YEARS ON THE BENCH

No matter that you call them rail fans, rail buffs, train watchers or railroad camp followers, the legions of those fond of trains are as diverse as America itself. They range from the casual delight of grandparent and grandchild sharing a steam train ride to the thoroughly rail smitten who attend conventions and engage in period rail reenactments. Their ranks include those of humble origin and the high born.

Rail employees do not always know what to make of this following, alternating between responses of amusement, bemusement, aggravation, and toleration. Most railroad workers are at heart rail fans too. It's just that in that intensely blue-collar world it's unseemly to lose the stoic look or let the bosses take advantage of workers' fondness for the work.

The annals of train watching contain many examples of dedication and persistence. Often it is an avocation picked up in childhood and sustained into the twilight of life. Rail employees marvel at those cases of longevity, for they often bracket a railroad worker's career duration. Veteran train watchers are often known by name, or at least by description, to railroad workers within a certain territory.

So it was that a retired Great Northern engineer steered me to a man he called "the greatest living rail fan in North America." Roscoe chuckled at that description when I contacted him at his assisted-living apartment in Grand Forks, North Dakota. But he did not disavow the title.

Spent fifty good years watching trains from the bench. It may not sound like an accomplishment, but I enjoyed myself and learned a lot. If you're like most people, you can't say the same about the old folks you know. I call them "senile citizens." They're cranky 'cause life passed them by. Well, yes the world does move along and eventually it moves along without us. If you watch trains you figure that out by the time you're ten years old.

My wife never did understand my love for trains. But, like the wives of card players, bowlers, fishermen, and drinkers, she learned to tolerate it.

I think she liked to see me enjoy myself and didn't mind getting me out of her kitchen. She's gone now, ten years this autumn.

You could say I've watched trains almost 90 years. I was real steady at it for 50. Some called me dedicated, some called me organized, and some just called me crazy. Most would just notice me and say, "There goes Roscoe with his train ledger." Some would laugh, but most didn't. Maybe because of the old doctor in town when I was a boy. When someone would remark that my hobby was strange, he would just say, "The boy is taking measure of America."

He was right. I did get a sense about this country that you couldn't get easily in Grand Forks. You barely needed to read a newspaper or listen to a radio if you knew what to look for on the trains or eavesdrop on passengers and railroaders. It was all there, our pride and our pain. You just had to look and listen.

My main years were from 1922 to 1972. In 1922 I was just starting to write longhand, instead of printing. By 1972 the Great Northern was gone and Amtrak had started. Good years for train watching and good years for me. It's all in my train ledger, the dates, times, car numbers. I did a little almost every day, no matter what came in the way of cold or storm.

For the first few years that I watched, the Great Northern ran numbered passenger trains. The names came a bit later. At least that's what the old schedules reflect. By the middle of the 1920s along came the Oriental Limited and Glacier Park Limited. Those were the pride of the Great Northern and some of the best passenger trains to ever cross this country.

By the late 1920s and early 1930s there was expanded passenger service. We really felt like we were a major stop by then. We had the Day Limited, Night Express, Red River Valley Express, and the Oriental Limited. Then, in the 1930s, came the Fast Mail and the Empire Builder. Not everybody remembers that the Empire Builder did not always come through Grand Forks. There were some years, especially in World War II, when the Empire Builder used the Surrey Cutoff.

In the 1940s they rolled out the Alexandrian and Red River Limited. My ledger tells only half the story in those times. Those little disturbances in Europe and the Pacific threw off a lot of personal timetables. Draft board couldn't decide what to do about me. First they wanted me, then they didn't, then they took me, and after they took me midway through the war, with a crop of boys ten years my junior, they blew my knee out on maneuvers in Texas and sent me home.

The Red River Limited was upgraded in the 1950s and they added the Dakotan. In the 1960s the lineup was the Red River Limited, the Western Star, and the Winnipeg Limited. With the 1970s came the changeover. First, the merger and "rising" of the Burlington Northern Western Star. Next the Amtrak resurrection of the Empire Builder.

Those were some important years in American history and good times in Grand Forks, despite some hard years. You could see the economic cycles in the trains. In prosperity, they picked up service to Canada—the tourists, and the hunters and fishermen. In depression, shorter trains and the revival of the mixed trains of passengers and freight. In war, the troop trains. And, with the four-lane highways, the end of branch line passenger service.

People often think of Grand Forks only in terms of transcontinental rail travel, a link to the Pacific Northwest. But our history is richer than that. We started railroad life on the old St. Paul, Minneapolis, & Manitoba in 1879. This was frontier then! Old men told about coming out here by those first trains and seeing Indian war parties, cavalry, and covered wagons along the way.

The genuine transcontinental part of our train service came to pass in the 1890s. That's when real passenger service, without benefit of cattle cars and freight, was instituted with brand new equipment. Soon we had scheduled service to Duluth, Winnipeg, St. Paul, and the Pacific Northwest. The old-timers told me it was an exciting time, the old times mixing with the modern era. Homesteaders riding along with businessmen, mining speculators, cattle buyers, timber barons, inventors, gunslingers, cowboys, and Indian chiefs.

In my youth the novel train was the Glacier Park Limited. The whole idea of tourists was novel. We gawked at those rich people from back east more than they gawked at us. Sometimes we sold them things on their brief stops. Sometimes they would take a layover to sample local life. Some were high and mighty. Some told wonderful stories of their world travels. It made the world seem more neighborly.

As for me, I only ever went more than twenty miles from here on three occasions, all three times by train. Once to Minot. Then off to the service. And finally when the grandkids sent me an Amtrak ticket to the Twin Cities. That was really something!

HONEYMOON TRAIN

In times of prosperity, rail travel was the standard mode of travel for newlyweds headed to a honeymoon destination. The practice became entrenched when the railroads recognized the revenue potential of scheduled service to resort areas. As the nineteenth century drew to a close it was possible for brides and grooms to travel in comfort to most seaside communities, mountain retreats, and pastoral spas.

With the advent of more comfortable sleeping compartments and more upscale dining cars, the train itself came to be viewed as the honeymoon site. Upper-crust newlyweds could tour the entire continent, striking strange Victorian-era poses such as buffalo shooting from the rear platform of their car or meeting with Lakota chiefs in full regalia. The Midwest's more modestly well-off made do with rail tours of the lake country to the north and west of Chicago.

That was the hope of our Waukegan, Illinois, informant, a great-grandmother of New England stock. But as happened with so many lives, World War II intervened and altered her envisioned honeymoon train.

Jim and I were both easterners, he of Philadelphia and I of Hartford. He was a Princeton classmate of my older brother. He started courting me right under my parents' noses without them even catching on. I was sixteen and he was a dashing twenty-one-year-old senior graduating as the war clouds gathered. We planned to elope as soon as I turned eighteen and take a honeymoon by train. The war threw our schedule off considerably.

Jim ended up in the naval aviator program, flew off carriers soon after Pearl Harbor, and I didn't hear from him for months at a time. More than once, upon reading about those great battles of the South Pacific, I assumed him dead. In early 1944 he was sent to the Great Lakes Naval Station to train cadets. I wanted to get on a train to Chicago immediately. But wartime travel was not simple. It took me months to plot my trip on a series of local trains, commuters, and trolleys until I made it to Chicago.

My head was filled with visions. I thought I was destined to be a refined officer's wife entertaining in Chicago society. I imagined a train honeymoon up to Green Lake, Wisconsin, a spot a pastor's wife commended to me. This was already a compromise from my dream of a honeymoon in the Berkshires, back east. But it was wartime and I knew that nineteen-year-old girls could not reorganize the world to their liking.

It took me days to hook up with Jim. I was so innocent, I expected to walk onto the base and look him up. Instead I spent days in a seedy boardinghouse until he rescued me, smothered me with kisses, and gave me the bad news. He was transferred again, to leave within forty-eight hours, leading a group of new aviators to Texas for final orientation and deployment overseas.

So we had to move fast and break a few rules. We were married in the Great Lakes chapel at 10:30 A.M. and were boarding the train to Texas at 3:15 P.M. It was a mixed train of three civilian passenger coaches, a dining car, a club car, several baggage cars, and a string of old troop coaches. At boarding I was hit with my next surprise. I was so naive that I thought that my dependent's pass, itself a dubious exercise in creative writing, would entitle me to ride along with Jim.

Instead the Shore Patrol pried me loose of my new husband and escorted me to the passenger coaches. Jim shouted that we'd talk in Springfield and I tried to stop crying. I settled into the trip, but I was unhappy. This was most definitely not the honeymoon of my dreams. Never mind that it was spartan and lacking amenities. It didn't even compensate with the rollicking mischief that young people use to overcome adversity. If I couldn't be a train debutante, I at least wanted to be a daffy Lucille Ball.

The conductor told us that we started off on Illinois Central tracks. Somewhere south of the city we were rerouted eastward into Indiana. We must have covered four hundred miles of track in order to get to Springfield, stopping, adding more cars, and dropping off a few. We pulled into Springfield considerably after anticipated arrival. It was then that I first learned that the troop coaches had been switched out of our train and coupled into a larger southbound troop train.

So there I was in Springfield. No money, no copy of Jim's travel orders, no luggage or change of clothes. My only fig leaf was the doctored dependent's pass. Upon reboarding, the new conductor arched an eyebrow at the pass. Fortunately, a brassy farm wife piped up. "Her husband's military car was taken out of the train and rerouted," she said in my defense.

By morning we were in St. Louis where, so everyone told me, the matter would be straightened out and I would rejoin Jim. In St. Louis I explained my circumstances. It was all chalked up to wartime confusion, as if it had happened a thousand times before. Railroad agents told me that the troop train had been rerouted behind us and was due within an hour. At that point I didn't know what to believe.

When that troop train arrived in St. Louis, I turned into a girl on a mission. I started boarding the cars, looking for Jim. This, I can assure you, set off quite a response. The conductors called the Shore Patrol, the Military Police, the railroad detectives, and the St. Louis police. They claimed I nearly set off a riot. I begged to differ. There were wolf whistles, hurrahs, and some rather racy invitations, but it was more comical than threatening.

My only objective was to find Jim. I suppose it seemed like I was making a big fuss. I certainly was prone to tears at that age. Remember, I was a nineteen-year-old bride from a sheltered and comfortable background. Perhaps I was acting a bit childish. Perhaps I was disturbing military routine and protocol. Goodness sakes, I had been married less than twenty four hours, and it seemed like the entire federal apparatus was conspiring to keep me from my husband.

The various authorities were in dispute over what to do with me. At one point the Shore Patrol was pulling my arm one way while the St. Louis police were pulling the other arm another way. I might have been injured had not some naval aviators waded in to pry me loose. The ultimate rescue came in the form of a gruff old marine gunnery sergeant.

The ribbons on the gunny's chest bespoke service in World War I and the banana wars of Central America. As he waded into our little melee, he explained he was babysitting an admiral traveling in a private car. We were disturbing the admiral, he explained. He said the admiral wished to know what the disturbance was about. So I told the story, starting from the point when my brother brought Jim home to Connecticut when I was sixteen.

The gunny winked and walked back to the admiral's car. He soon returned and led me away through a sea of amazed faces. He placed me in an empty train compartment and locked me in. I was indignant. I pounded on the door and shouted to be let out. Within minutes the gunny opened to door and pushed Jim in the compartment. It turned out the admiral was traveling to Corpus Christi and his car would be part of our train.

So that was our honeymoon train. There in an admiral's private car in a tiny compartment with a single width berth, a scratchy wool navy blanket on starched sheets, and an old pug-faced gunnery sergeant for a steward. But he was a good steward at that. Brought drinks and sandwiches to the compartment and ushered us to breakfast with the admiral the next morning.

Was it my dream honeymoon? No, it was far from what I envisioned. Still, I would not trade the life it began for anything. In the 51 years from war bride to widow there were many challenges. Jim built up a career in Chicago in the airline industry after the war. We raised a family and did quite well. But his health depleted many of our resources when he retired.

We did get in a train trip for our fiftieth anniversary. It was part second honeymoon and part trip to a navy reunion in San Diego. It was much more comfortable than the single berth. It was romantic too, since it brought back memories of the train from Chicago to Texas. On the way to San Diego we met a young newlywed couple from Peoria. I'll save their story for another time.

RUNAWAY TRAIN

Errant trains have been fodder for amusing and horrifying stories since the beginning of railroads. Trains have had various ways of escaping the custody of their crews, especially in the early stages of developing rail technologies. There is perhaps no more embarrassing turn of events to rail management than a train that got away.

This is to be distinguished from lesser calamities such as missing cars, rolling stock that literally rolls away, and the fabled children's story of the caboose that got loose. No, the subject here is the fully constituted train, under power, which contrives to continue its journey without benefit of humans. Each era of railroading possesses a few representative stories of this type.

The line of stories begins with the weak prototype engines, which were sometimes assisted by crew and passengers alike pushing them over the crests of difficult hills. Alas, some of those trains continued their downhill path without these assistants. In the Old West more than one payroll-bearing train had its crew evicted by bandits while it continued its travels. In the days of diesel, engineers have keeled over and brakemen have fallen off.

A variety of mechanisms are supposed to prevent such things. But as the following tale suggests, technology is not always up to the task. Lois, a farm wife from western Nebraska, tells the story from ground level.

I never heard of a runaway train before. I thought that was just something out of movies or cartoons. But truth is not only stranger than fiction, it's stranger than science fiction. At least that's my conclusion after my conversation with the Union Pacific about remote-control trains.

I was mad as a wet hen when it almost hit me at a dark crossing. There I was in the truck cab, loaded with kids, the dog, and a sleeping husband. We were coming back from Willow Island. Rick, my husband, had a few beers with his buddies and I was taking a turn at the wheel. They were all asleep except the dog.

Everyone realizes that you can't have gates at every farm crossing in America. Even lights don't always help. In rural areas you tend to ignore lights when half the time they're flashing and there's no train in sight. Well, at least at night, lights get you to look. That might have helped me that night.

But it came through our crossing at full speed. I was barely able to stop in time before the lead car zoomed right through. I hit the brakes so hard that it jerked Rick tight in the shoulder belt. He sure woke up in a hurry and was wide-eyed from a look at a train zipping past a few feet in front of our headlights.

The kids started crying and the dog became agitated. I tried to explain to Rick that there was no whistle and the train was unlit on the end that barreled through. First, he had to exhaust a built-up string of profanities. Then he was able to remember that I am a careful driver and that farmers and ranchers have had over a century of trouble with the Union Pacific.

We said a prayer of thanks when we got home that night. The next day we heard stories from neighbors and some reports on the radio. So I called the Union Pacific and demanded an explanation. I called toll free numbers and private extensions that I wheedled out of secretaries. I called operations centers and managers on their mobile phones. From all that runaround I did piece together a picture of what happened.

It all started, apparently, with one of those train actions that anger drivers everywhere. In farm and ranch country, the Union Pacific is famous for leaving trains in the crossings for hours at a time. It often happens—and apparently did this time—that a driver blocked from his homestead will take exception to this situation. They often take matters into their own hands. I've seen country people pull a line of railroad cars out of the way with a tractor. The Union Pacific told me that in this case someone decoupled part of the train. I didn't know that could happen and still have the left-behind part of the train move. That's when they told me about remote-control trains. Something about "helper" engines in the back part of the train operated electronically by an engineer in the lead part.

So the way this worked when the train started moving again was that a gap developed between the two sections. By the time the train got to our crossing there was a ten-mile gap in the train. On the lead car of the back section there were no lights, no air horns, not even reflective panels that might have stood out as we approached the crossing. No, it was just sixty black cars barreling through the dark.

They said that the train went over fifty miles in this condition. That's at least three dozen crossings in the section we're talking about. That includes streets in towns and some well-traveled highways, not just dirt and farm lanes. They said they stopped as soon as they knew. They said it was just a fluke. That would be small consolation if someone had been killed.

Recently I was a chaperone on a school trip. We took the kids to the Pony Express Museum at Gothenburg. One of the volunteers there talked about transportation in this part of the country. He talked to the kids about the Spanish horses that the Indians adopted. He talked about early travel on the Missouri River. He talked about Lewis and Clark and how our area became the connection between both sides of the continent. And he talked about the railroads.

According to him, the coming of the railroads signaled the beginning of the modern era in Nebraska. It was the way cattle and grain moved to market. He even kept the kids entertained with notions about how one day there would be trains on the Moon and Mars. How they would be robot trains loaded with ore from mines. How they would be operated by signals from satellites.

I thought he was just telling a tall tale for the benefit of the kids. I had no idea that the Union Pacific was working on the same idea on Earth.

RIVER CITY LAYOUT

Many a railroad fantasy has been nurtured by modeling in the various hobbyist scales. Model railroading cuts across most class and ethnic divisions in America. The pursuit allows for a number of different interest levels and financial commitments.

Some collect antique toy trains. Some pride themselves on the completeness of their model equipment, treasuring all available rolling stock of one railroad or another. Others focus on particular railroad periods or settings.

Like other hobbies, model railroading produces a subculture of devotees that has its own quirks and rules. This subculture can be viewed from a number of angles. It is often looked at in terms of a preservation perspective and linked to a glorious golden age. Others depict it is as the most authentic blue-collar hobby. A few detractors look at it as a Rust Belt variation on the Trekkie phenomenon.

Among those with large fixed layouts there is often an attempt to re-create a slice of railroad life that holds some sentimental value to the modeler. It might be a grandfather's rail yard or an idealized representation of a particular era. For Martin, it is a slice of a treasured boyhood that can still be easily imagined from his Victorian home on a hilltop in Dubuque, Iowa.

Believe it or not, Dubuque was a premier rail town in its day. A half dozen of the pioneer lines from Chicago and Milwaukee set Dubuque as an early goal in their western vision. By the peak time of railroading, four of the giants called on the pretty River City.

That's what this layout you're looking at is modeled after. I call it Little River City. That's why it's got four separate track arrangements. It's meant to represent the Burlington, the Great Western, the Milwaukee Road, and the Illinois Central. Few towns of Dubuque size were as jammed up with trains.

You can see how terrain really packed things together. The hills, the river, and the city itself interact to make for an unusual layout. It's a good mix of industrial and residential with an old city feel. Look at the unusual features: incline track on the hill, warehouses, docks, elevators, and lots of early intermodel features. It was one of the first places to have interaction between trains, barges, and trucking. Then the scenery, with the hilltop houses, the seminaries, the churches, and the old business district.

Now you might think I'm drawn to this particular configuration because I've been looking at this piece of real estate for over fifty years. It's true that this drafty old perch overlooking my hometown provides lots of memories and inspiration. But it's more than that. Just because I had a boyhood and adolescence tied to these scenes doesn't mean that I've fallen into sentimental patterns and technical ease.

I know of no other layout that is based on Mississippi River railroading that runs simulations on both sides of the river. I haven't seen many that rival mine for number of crossings and interlockings. There are four major points of intersection and I have them close to spatial scale. Let me take you on the tour.

Here's the Wood Interlocking, the meeting point of the Illinois Central and the Milwaukee Road. Because I'm basically using a 1943 setting, there's a holdup of meat waiting for flats of military machinery to go through. Sometimes I'll stage my derailments there and bring in my mobile crane. I also have IC work cars, with the gondolas, rail flats, and bunk cars that I use to create a scene of rebuilding the interlocking.

Over here is the Milwaukee and Great Western crossing, which was thought of as part of the complex just to the east called Dubuque Junction. It really wasn't, since it did serve the bridge as the junction did. It doesn't have the history of collisions and derailments that some crossings do. But it was an interesting spot in its day for watching train movements.

Dubuque Junction, now there's a rail tangle! I spent a lot of my youth there in the company of other delinquents, making a pest of myself, and running afoul of the local authorities. I wasn't born to a house on the hill. I ran with the gully urchins and we had a gang that practically lived at Dubuque Junction.

It's just a shame that I can't re-create my favorite scenes from Dubuque Junction. Well, I can put the equipment in place, but not the human sights and sounds. Dubuque Junction had more interaction between workers of other railroads than just about anyplace I remember. Always joking back and forth, good-natured insults, and yelling about who was the best. In tie-ups, I saw them play cards together, play catch with a baseball, throw snowballs, and sing dirty songs. Sometimes they would bring the biggest and dumbest section hands from their respective railroads down to the junction for some boxing, with plenty of betting, of course. I can't get all that on a model train layout, but it sure brings it all back for me.

Dubuque Junction was home to just about anything and everything that could happen when you have multiple railroads in play. The place figured into just about anything that happened out on the bridge. Look at how they mesh into each other. If the junction is tied up, then the bridge is as good as out, and if the bridge is tangled up, the junction is useless.

Now across the river you've got the flip side of that with the East Cabin Interlocking. The same railroads—the IC, the Great Western, and the Burlington—part company to make their ways into Illinois and Wisconsin. And, of course, that figured into IC and Burlington passenger service over in East Dubuque. See, there are the stations.

Also on the east side of the river, you've got the IC tunnel there on the hill. That entrance isn't quite right, the portal angle is off because I'm dealing with a loop that hooks into my Burlington track. The real tunnel was a dandy and the scene of many shenanigans. There was a time when it served as sort of a lovers' lane for the young and reckless. Hard to imagine, but more than one young fellow got his first kiss in there. Almost the same number scared the bejeebers out of their girlfriends by clearing the tunnel one step ahead of IC freights.

Down here you can see my representation of Dubuque Packing. That was a hefty chunk of rail traffic back in those days. It's an interesting side feature to have an industry of that size on a layout. But it's not as big a deal as a layout that incorporates a major stockyard complex, like Omaha or Kansas City. Dubuque Packing is like Dubuque Junction in a way, it brings back memories of workers and hangers-on.

You can see the other odds and ends for yourself. There are some trolleys, but these aren't exactly historically accurate. I tried to do the business of Terminal Street and some of the old railroad hangouts, beer joints, and cafes. The downtown and the riverfront have changed so much from what I have here. Don't get me wrong, redevelopment is a blessing to areas that are totally blighted. Age alone does not make a wreck of a building significant.

But I keep this layout to remind me of those rail days and the way of life that went with them. So when I hear of interlopers like Canadian National, I & M Rail Link, and Chicago Central I can be the old grouch who growls, "I remember real railroading in River City."

LINCOLN'S DEPOT

Railroad depots and stations figured in many historical events during the last half of the nineteenth century and the first half of the twentieth century. Many a dignitary uttered pithy projections of civic undertakings from depot thresholds. Many a conquering hero basked in adulation on the platforms of hometown stations.

The great rail cathedrals of the urban centers soared in majesty and harkened to Europe with forms Romanesque or Gothic. They staked their positions and their principles with names like "central" and "union." Rural travelers encountering them for the first time stood in awe.

Truth be known, many of the more poignant moments of rail-related history happened in far more modest surroundings. Great characters on the American stage often began their journeys from the handhewn rail shacks at whistle-stops, standing nervously with satchels amid crates of freight. Soldiers-to-be frequently began careers that would later end in acclaim on foreign shores in a scene of humble patience by the tracks on a windswept prairie.

Those rooted in the Midwest know that there is one archetypal American character who best represents everything both humble and heroic. None so rooted would express surprise that such a story would be found in Springfield, Illinois. Hank, son of a Great Western engineer, will give us a tour of depots that is at once historical and sociological.

This was the Great Western Depot. Now, appropriately, it is the Lincoln Depot. This is the site that frames the most intense period in the life of the most quintessentially American man ever produced on this continent. Maybe the first man to really think as an American.

Lincoln gave his farewell address to the people of Springfield and Illinois from this site. He did not set foot here again. This is where he returned in his casket in 1865. The things in between are widely known and will be known as long as there are free men.

The depot stands for everything in that time and everything that flowed from that time. To me, it's an emblem of a reforged and tempered country. It's a sign of endurance. It's a symbol of a burly nation on the move. And it's the representative depot that reminds us of all the joy and pain that accompanied the farewells and homecomings of the wars and other great upheavals. I hear those things in these walls and feel them in this ground.

I realize that every depot, station, and whistle-stop lean-to has a history, many of them proud to the core. We're just luckier than most to have one that played a role in the life of the greatest man of the people produced by any republic. It's more than a depot, it's a shrine.

That's not to say that other railroad stations are not also shrines in their own way. There's a revival all over the country to spiff these buildings up, to restore them to their grandeur and to let them reclaim their place in the community. Though I often side with the preservation purists, I'm for anything that gives these buildings a second lease on life. If a depot faces the choice between becoming a brew pub or facing the wrecking ball, I'm all for letting the suds flow.

I've seen quite a few adapted to fine restaurants, professional buildings, and community centers. A few people with deep pockets are even ambitious enough to turn them into homes. They make great museums for local historical societies. Not to mention the handful of farsighted municipal officials with the instinct to keep the buildings in the public domain as a bet on the return of some sort of commuter rail. In the meantime, if they can serve senior citizens and the handicapped as van centers, so much the better.

I just hope that those who restore the depots go beyond bricks and mortar. They really need to understand passenger facilities as living and breathing history. They need to research the affiliated railroad, understand the schedules, know the local chronology of events, identify the local personalities, and appreciate the evolution of the facility over the period of its use.

Then you should put out the call for the artifacts. Let the oldsters empty their attics and their ancient traveling trucks. Clean up the old railroad tools, reframe the old photographs, display the railroad china and linen, and polish those conductor badges. Any town worth its salt can fill several display cases with the railroad paraphernalia that grew legs and walked away from the original proprietors.

Once you assemble the facts and the material artifacts you're in a position to delve into the trickier stuff, like the moods and lore that resonate in a railroad place. You're in myth and magic territory when you've reached that point. I discovered that right here in the Lincoln Depot. A good half dozen times I've encountered visitors who were drawn here by old family stories originating elsewhere. Most involved Lincoln's funeral train as it passed through the eastern states and how their grandfathers or great-grandfathers went to the local train station to pay their respects.

What drew them here? In many cases their local depot was gone. Or development pressures had totally transformed the area. So I guess they come here to capture the feeling of that time and to stand at the end of that sad journey.

If you tune in you can feel that time. Visualize the two waiting rooms of those days, one for women and one for men. In the women's waiting room there are small children and the cooing of babies. In the men's waiting room excited boys run in and out while fathers flick cigar ashes into buckets or discreetly drip juice into spittoons. The mood would be somber on the day Lincoln's body returned. A crowd would be assembling. Disabled veterans would be shown places to sit. Soldiers in blue and freed slaves in rags alike would be weeping. Imagine a scene of flags and black crepe. Listen to the soft respectful murmurs and the expressions of concern for the future. Think of that moment when heads lift and turn at the sound of that train whistle. Lincoln's coming home!

SOME RAILROADING TERMS

Ash Pit: A hole between the rails where steam locomotive ashes are dumped for cleaning.

Blackbearded: The practice of painting over a prior line's logo, insignia, and numbers after rolling stock transferred in ownership.

Carbody Locomotive: A lightweight locomotive usually built for community passenger service or short hauls.

Carman: A maintenance mechanic for all rolling stock other than locomotives, freight, passenger, welder, and wrecking crew specialties.

Center Key: A massive steel piece that holds the coupler in the centersill.

Centersill: The central structural beam that runs the length of a car and contains both couplers.

Chessie: Chesapeake & Ohio Railroad; also the name of its kitten logo.

Coal Tender: A fuel-bearing car directly behind a steam locomotive.

Comealong: A pulling and lifting tool; also called chain jack, cable jack, or hand winch.

Cowcatcher: A wedge or flange in front of a locomotive just above rail level.

Deadhead: A rider without assignment, usually a railroad employee catching a ride but not a member of the crew.

Drawbar: The entire coupler assembly: coupler, knuckle, yoke, and center key.

Drover: A cowboy or cattle driver who loads, unloads, and cares for livestock being transported by railroad.

Engine Trucks: The wheel assemblies under a locomotive.

F-7: Locomotive type.

Gondola: An open bulk material car that often carries scrap metal or railroad ties.

Grab Iron: A metal rod or rail on railroad equipment that serves as a ladder or step.

Hogshead: An engineer.

Hospital Train: Usually a train made up of damaged cars; in wartime, a military medical train.

Hostler: A roundhouse worker who moves and positions locomotives.

Hotbox: A journal box that has caught fire or is throwing sparks.

Journal Bearing: A half-bearing on rolling stock that bears the weight of the car directly on top of the axle.

Journal Box: The part of the wheel truck that encases axle ends and bearings.

Maintenance of Way: Track, bridge, and crossing repair.

Milwaukee Shops: The Milwaukee Road's main repair facility in Milwaukee, unique in the number of cars actually constructed there.

Pin Lifter: A metal arm that allows a worker to decouple cars without getting between cars.

Relettered: Changes in logo or nomenclature.

Ribside: Steel construction style on some railroad equipment.

Ribsider: A nickname for a 1940s or 1950s caboose out of the Milwaukee Shops.

Rip Track: A maintenance area in a rail yard where carmen repair cars.

Road-switcher: A switch engine used for multiple tasks or retired from freight service.

Sand House: A building near the roundhouse where engines are resupplied with sand for traction purposes.

Side Bearings: A part that prevents side-to-side rocking on boxcars.

Switch Key: A standardized heavy brass key that opens manually operated track switches.

Switch Point: A narrow leading edge of rail in a switch that catches the wheels and turns them.

Switch Stand: The upright portion of a manual track switch where the handle is located.

Through Train: A train that does not stop at all stations or depots.

Tie Pole: A raw log to be made into a railroad tie.

Unit Train: A freight train made up of one type of car hauling one type of commodity (e.g., a coal train going to a power plant).

Way Freight: A branch line freight that stops to drop off and pick up cars.

MORE GREAT TITLES FROM TRAILS BOOKS

ACTIVITY GUIDES

Paddling Southern Wisconsin: 82 Great Trips by Canoe and Kayak
Mike Svob

Paddling Northern Wisconsin: 82 Great Trips by Canoe and Kayak
Mike Svob

Paddling Illinois: 64 Great Trips by Canoe and Kayak
Mike Svob

Wisconsin Golf Getaways: A Guide to More Than 200 Great
Courses and Fun Things to Do
Jeff Mayers and Jerry Poling

Wisconsin Underground: A Guide to Caves, Mines, and Tunnels in
and around the Badger State,
Doris Green

Great Wisconsin Walks: 45 Strolls, Rambles, Hikes, and Treks,
Wm. Chad McGrath

Great Minnesota Walks: 49 Strolls, Rambles, Hikes, and Treks,
Wm. Chad McGrath

Best Wisconsin Bike Trips
Phil Van Valkenberg

TRAVEL GUIDES

Great Minnesota Weekend Adventures
Beth Gauper

Tastes of Minnesota: A Food Lover's Tour
Donna Tabbert Long

Great Indiana Weekend Adventures
Sally McKinney

Historical Wisconsin Getaways: Touring the Badger State's Past
Sharyn Alden

The Great Wisconsin Touring Book: 30 Spectacular Auto Tours
Gary Knowles

Wisconsin Family Weekends: 20 Fun Trips for You and the Kids
Susan Lampert Smith

County Parks of Wisconsin, Revised Edition
Jeannette and Chet Bell

Up North Wisconsin: A Region for All Seasons
Sharyn Alden

The Spirit of Door County: A Photographic Essay
Darryl R. Beers

Great Wisconsin Taverns: 101 Distinctive Badger Bars
Dennis Boyer

Great Wisconsin Restaurants
Dennis Getto

Great Weekend Adventures
the Editors of Wisconsin Trails

The Wisconsin Traveler's Companion: A Guide to Country Sights
Jerry Apps and Julie Sutter-Blair

HOME AND GARDEN

Creating a Perennial Garden in the Midwest
Joan Severa

Bountiful Wisconsin: 110 Favorite Recipes
Terese Allen

Foods That Made Wisconsin Famous
Richard J. Baumann

HISTORICAL GUIDES

Walking Tours of Wisconsin's Historic Towns
Lucy Rhodes, Elizabeth McBride, and Anita Matcha

Wisconsin: The Story of the Badger State
Norman K. Risjord

Barns of Wisconsin
Jerry Apps

Portrait of the Past:
A Photographic Journey Through Wisconsin, 1865–1920
Howard Mead, Jill Dean, and Susan Smith

FOR YOUNG PEOPLE

Wisconsin Portraits: 55 People Who Made a Difference
Martin Hintz

ABCs of Wisconsin
Dori Hillestad Butler and Alison Relyea

W Is for Wisconsin
Dori Hillestad Butler and Eileen Dawson

OTHER TITLES OF INTEREST

The I-Files: True Reports of Unexplained Phenomena in Illinois
Jay Rath

The W-Files: True Reports of Wisconsin's Unexplained Phenomena
Jay Rath

The M-Files: True Reports of Minnesota's Unexplained Phenomena
Jay Rath

FOR A FREE CATALOG
PHONE, WRITE, OR E-MAIL US.
Trails Books
P.O. Box 317
Black Earth, WI 53515
(800) 236-8088 • e-mail: info@wistrails.com
www.trailsbooks.com